EASY-TO-MAKE WOODEN TOYS

EASY-TO-MAKE
WOODEN TOYS

TERRY FORDE

GUILD PUBLISHING
LONDON

This edition published 1985 by
Book Club Associates
by arrangement with
David & Charles (Publishers) Ltd

Printed in Great Britain

CONTENTS

FOREWORD

The intention of this book is to show that making practical, sturdy wooden toys is easy, pleasurable and inexpensive, and to encourage those with minimal experience to have a go.

Unfortunately first timers usually don't have scrap wood lying around the house, they don't have tool kits and above all they are inexperienced. In order to make it as simple as possible, all the toys in this book are made from plywood and wherever practical only one thickness per toy is used, usually ¼in or ½in. This will make the purchasing much easier and cheaper. The cost becomes prohibitive if it becomes necessary to buy chisels, planes, saws, clamps, etc in order to make only one toy. I have therefore made all the toys in this book using the bare minimum of tools. Anyone with additional tools will probably be able to make the toys more quickly and more easily, but for the person with more time than money extra tools are not essential to make a good toy.

A major problem with tools is that they need sharpening. A craftsman never begrudges the time spent sharpening his tools and only beginners attempt to work with blunt tools and make everything much harder for themselves. Because sharpening tools correctly is a skill in itself and requires practice I have chosen tools which do not require sharpening and are simple to use.

As for experience — well there's no substitute. It is certainly better to be competent with one tool than incompetent with a complete workshop, so I have chosen the fretsaw (or jigsaw, as it is known in America) as the only tool which needs to be mastered for these toys. It is the ideal tool to begin working with as it is quiet, clean and can be used on the kitchen table. It is also fairly inexpensive to buy and never needs sharpening because the blades are thrown away when blunt. Another advantage is that using the fretsaw (jigsaw) does not require great strength which makes this an excellent tool for any beginner whether man, woman or child, or even partially disabled. Every toy shown has been made by me using only the tools mentioned and the methods described.

Rather than go into long boring detail on the comparative adhesive strengths of various glues or why the wood of one tree has more advantageous properties than that of another, I will merely state the materials I used and leave you either to follow suit or to use your own favourite material.

INTRODUCTION

Anyone who has ever read a DIY book will recognise this chapter immediately, indeed they may have already passed on to actually making the toys. This is the part of the book where tools, materials and techniques are discussed which tempted me to call it the 'Obligatory Boring Chapter'. In a perfect world someone would have written the definitive opening chapter for DIY books which could be issued separately to beginners as they purchased the book, rendering these chapters obsolete for ever more. This not being the perfect world, we are stuck with this chapter which, on reflection, is probably just as well. By limiting my choice of tools to essentials, some of my methods may well be considered unconventional and therefore need explanation. As this book is designed specifically to include the beginner this chapter will only deal with basics to avoid the confusion of choice. Naturally some of the methods are used repeatedly from toy to toy. To avoid repetition I intend to include these methods for windows, roofs, etc, here and refer back to them later during the actual toy-making.

Tools

Fretsaw (Jigsaw)

Known in England as a fretsaw, this tool is called a jigsaw in America. If you have never used a fretsaw (jigsaw) before, buy lots of blades as they break very easily. If you are breaking an inordinate number of blades you are probably twisting the blade around corners instead of sawing around them. Practice will overcome this but looking on the bright side at least they are not getting blunt. Remember that the teeth of the blade fit downwards in the saw and that the handle is held below the work being cut.

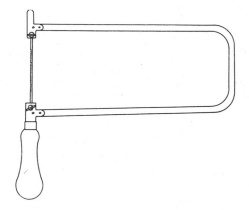

fig 1 Fretsaw

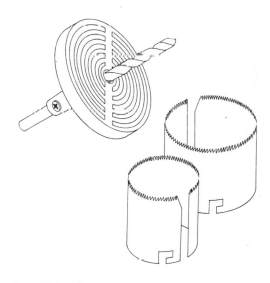

fig 2 Hole saw

Hole Saw

This is very effective for cutting out perfect circles. A hole saw consists of a drill bit with a cylindrical saw blade which attaches to it. They are usually sold complete with several different diameter blades and are very inexpensive.

Craft Knife

A sharp knife with a detachable blade which is easily replaced, extremely useful for scoring lines and cutting plastic tubing and cardboard.

Hammer

A small hammer would be better than a large one.

Drill

A hand drill is sufficient for all the toys, although many people have an electric drill these days. If you don't have one, it may be worth asking a friend or a neighbour to drill the holes for you as the number to be drilled is so small.

Files

I use these in lieu of a plane or a spoke-shave. Although they are not as good, they do produce the desired finish without needing to be sharpened and are ideal for finishing off the inside edge of the windows and doorways.

Without being silly and listing pencils and rulers, these are the only tools you will need.

Materials

Wood

All the toys are made from either ¼in or ½in ply and occasionally some small pieces of mouldings and dowelling. I prefer to use birch ply because it gives a first-class finish for either varnishing or painting. Birch ply is not the cheapest plywood but as only small quantities are required I think it is worth the extra cost involved.

Glue

I use Evo-Stick Resin 'W' wood glue for no better reason than that it sticks well and the nozzle on the bottle works better than any of the other brands I have tried.

Wood Filler

I usually use a waterproof filler to fill in the holes left by nails which have been punched below the surface. I prefer the waterproof type because it prevents the nails and panel pins from rusting and staining the paintwork.

Techniques

The one part of any DIY project which cannot be over-emphasised is accurate marking-out. It is pointless being able to cut to a line if the line is drawn in the wrong place. An old saying worth remembering is 'measure twice, cut once'.

Windows

To make a window, mark it out carefully, drill a hole through the centre and insert the fretsaw (jigsaw) blade through the hole. Then simply cut out the window pane and sand down any rough edges. Doors are made in the same way, although it is not usually necessary to drill a hole.

Roofs

I use two methods for roofs, one using a mitre joint (fig 3) and the other using a

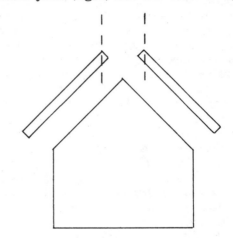

fig 3 Mitre joint

overlap ⟶

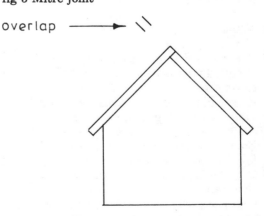

fig 4 Butt joint

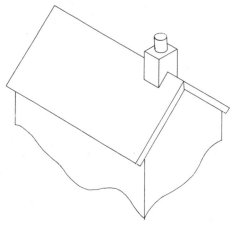

fig 5 Fixed roof with chimney

If the roof is to be fixed as in the case of the Farm or the Doll's House, glue and nail both sides on to the building (fig 5).

In the case of the Noah's Ark or the Castle where access through the roof is required, nail one side only of the roof on to the building. If you decide to use a butt joint, the shorter side should be the one to be nailed down. Two wooden strips are glued and nailed on to the underside of the loose section of the roof in order to keep it in place (fig 6).

Painting

The wood should be sanded smooth before painting and any nails should be punched below the surface and holes filled

½"x ½" wooden strips

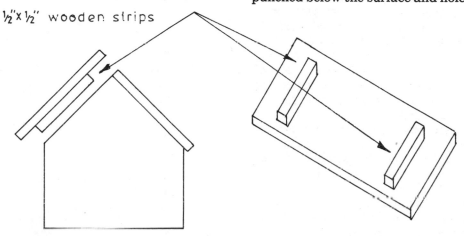

fig 6 Wooden strips to secure removeable side of roof in place

butt joint (fig 4). I think the mitre joint is more professional but children will not appreciate the difference so the easier butt joint may be used without qualms.

Mitre joint: Mark the wood as indicated by the dotted line in fig 3, then file down the waste wood carefully. On both types of joint one side of the roof should be nailed on to the house.

Butt joint: In the case of the butt joint, one side of the roof should be the thickness of the wood longer than the other; for example if one side of the roof is 4in deep and the timber used is ¼in thick, then the side with the overlap will be 4¼in deep.

with wood filler. Remember that any blemishes will be highlighted by the paint — not hidden by it. As the end product is to be given to a child, care must be taken to ensure that non-poisonous paints are used. If in doubt ask the supplier and, if still in doubt, use a different brand. I use Humbrol paints for painting small items such as soldiers because very small quantities can be bought and they are quick-drying, so more than one colour can be applied in one evening.

Paint is one of the areas I experiment with most. Sometimes paint shops reduce paint they can't sell so it is worth trying out new colour schemes. For instance, I once bought a tin of purple vinyl silk paint which would have looked hideous in

11

the lounge but on the toy garage it looked great. I now use vinyl silk wherever a glossy surface is not required because it has proved to be very hard-wearing and it withstands rigorous daily use.

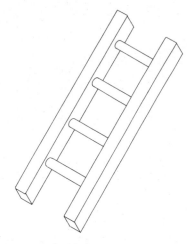

fig 7 A simple ladder

Dimensions

All the dimensions are given in inches as most tape measures are marked in this way rather than in feet and inches and the majority of people who are not involved with metric measurements during their working day are more familiar with the imperial system. However, for those who prefer metric equivalents, a conversion table is given opposite.

Only essential measurements have been included because beginners, when confronted with a drawing covered in measurements, don't know where to start and tend to progress around the drawing from one line to the next, losing sight of the overall picture and increasing the chances of error. It is far better to get the main sizes right and sort out the unimportant ones later. The unimportant sizes I am thinking of are the battlements on the Castles and the windows in the Farm, Cowboy Town, etc. As long as these are fairly symmetrical, the size is immaterial. The exception to this is the Georgian-style Doll's House where the windows are a feature of the house.

Ladders

These are easily made by using $\frac{3}{8} \times \frac{3}{8}$in wood and ¼in dowel. If you are not very accurate with a drill it may be wiser to use $\frac{1}{2} \times \frac{1}{2}$in wood. Cut the sides of the ladder to length, mark the position of the rungs (1¼in centres) and drill ¼in holes for the dowel. Cut the dowels to the required length (approximately 1½in) then glue them in position. Ladders can be made to any length and are useful for the Castles, Farm, Riverboat, Cowboy Town — in fact any toy that involves figures.

Conversion Table

inches	millimetres	inches	millimetres
⅛	3	4¼	108
¼	6	4½	114
⅜	10	4¾	121
½	13	5	127
¾	19	5½	140
1	25	6	152
1¼	32	6½	165
1½	38	7	178
1¾	44	7½	190
2	51	8	203
2¼	57	8½	216
2½	64	9	228
2¾	70	9½	241
3	76	10	254
3¼	83	10½	267
3½	89	11	279
3¾	95	11½	292
4	102	12	305

For those who prefer to work in metric, this conversion table provides guideline equivalent metric measurements.

REMOVALS VAN

(shown in colour on page 17)

This toy turned out to be far better than expected, because my children have discovered plenty of uses for it. It is used to transfer the doll's furniture from the town house to the summer palace. This was its intended function, but on top of that it is used as a skateboard, with the children standing on the roof, and as a sit-and-ride toy hurtling down our garden path. Mind you, I'm as daft as the children because I've had a go as well, so I can vouch for its strength.

Considering the treatment it receives, it is just as well that I fitted plastic wheels and a ¼in steel axle with spring-loaded hub-caps, which are generally available from hobby shops. I am certain that a wooden axle and wooden wheels would not have taken the strain.

1 Cut the sides, the base and the wheel arches of the van out of ⅜in ply. Two complete sets of front wheel arches are

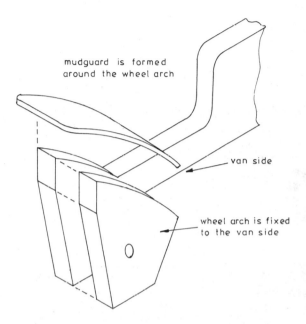

mudguard is formed around the wheel arch

van side

wheel arch is fixed to the van side

fig 1 Detail of front wheel arches with curved mudguard

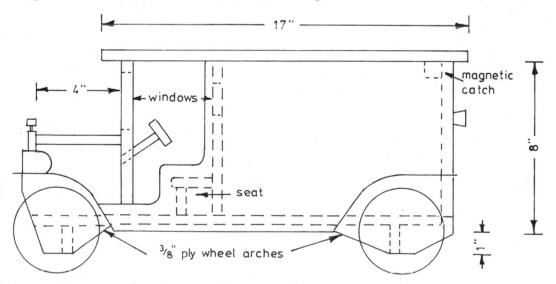

17"

4"

windows

magnetic catch

8"

1"

seat

⅜" ply wheel arches

fig 2 Side view and overall dimensions of van

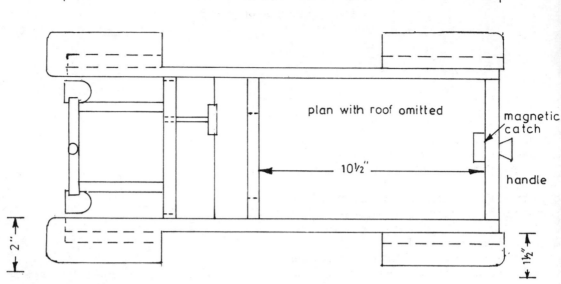

fig 3 Overhead view of van layout

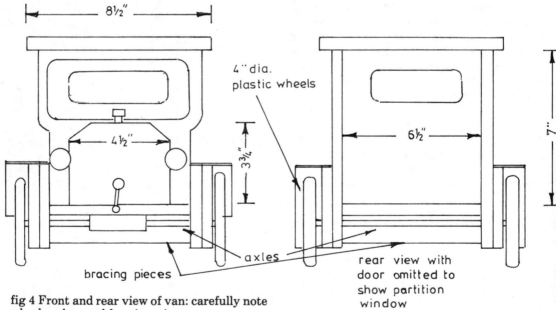

fig 4 Front and rear view of van: carefully note wheel arches and bracing pieces

needed. The extra set, fitted on top of the first set which is attached to the side of the van, is there to help with the bending of the mudguards. Drill ¼in holes in the wheel arches for the axles (fig 1).

2 Cut mudguards out of ⅛in ply and soak them in hot water. They can then be bent around the wheel arch and glued and nailed in place. Glue and nail the wheel arches to the sides of the van.

3 Make the bonnet out of three pieces of ⅜in ply and chamfer the top edges using a file. Strengthen it by fixing pieces of scrap wood inside it (see fig 5).

4 Cut out the radiator and drill a hole for the starting handle.

5 Make a radiator cap out of a circle of ⅜in ply, ½in in diameter. Drill a ¼in hole

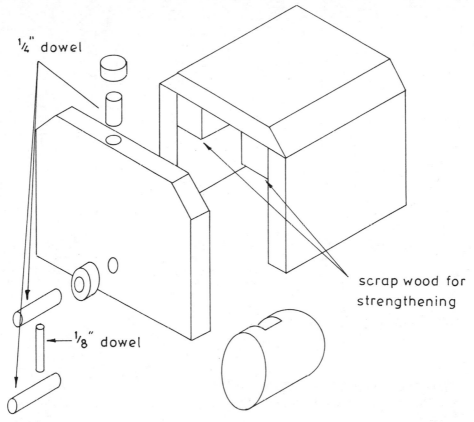

¼" dowel

⅛" dowel

scrap wood for strengthening

fig 5 Assembly details of the bonnet section with radiator cap and starting handle

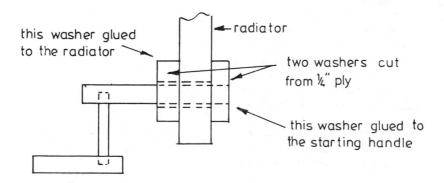

this washer glued to the radiator

radiator

two washers cut from ¼" ply

this washer glued to the starting handle

fig 6 Starting handle fitted through the radiator

15

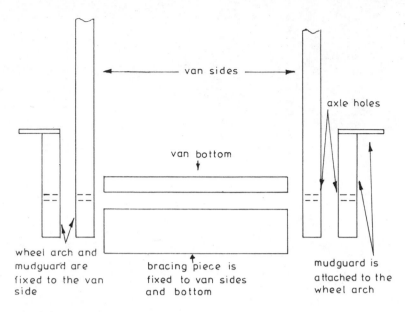

van sides

axle holes

van bottom

wheel arch and
mudguard are
fixed to the van
side

bracing piece is
fixed to van sides
and bottom

mudguard is
attached to the
wheel arch

fig 7 Positioning of bracing piece, axle, van
sides and wheel arches

in the cap and the top centre of the
radiator and join the two with a piece of
¼in dowel.
6 The starting handle needs two pieces of
¼in dowel and one piece of ⅛in dowel (see
the detailed diagram in fig 6). Drill two
holes in a piece of ⅜in ply and, using the
fretsaw, cut a circle around each hole.
7 Glue one of these pieces on to the ¼in
dowel. The other piece is glued to the
starting handle after it has been passed
through the radiator.
8 Fix the radiator to the bonnet.
9 Make headlights from 1in dowel. Round
off the backs with a file and sandpaper
before cutting them to length. Cut a ⅜in
notch in each one to slot over the radiator
and then cut off the front to the correct
length and glue them to the radiator (fig
5).
10 Cut out the windscreen section (see
Introduction, Windows) and drill a ¼in
hole at an angle for the steering column,
as can be seen in fig 2.
11 Make a steering wheel out of a 1in-
diameter circle of ¼in ply or 1in dowel,
glued to a piece of ¼in dowelling for the
steering wheel column. Glue it into the
dashboard.

Removals Van (page 13); Furniture (page 99);
Garage (page 20); Car Transporter (page 23);
Cars (page 28)

12 Attach the windscreen to the bonnet and the sides of the van to the floor. Cut out a partition to divide the front of the van from the back and make and attach the seat to it. Then fix the partition in place.

13 Fix two bracing pieces across the bottom of the van, close to the axle holes as fig 7 demonstrates.

14 Put the roof on and fit on a rear door with a hinge fitted to the floor of the van. A piano hinge with brass screws is the best. Make a little wooden handle for the door (fig 8), glue it on and fit a magnetic catch.

15 Finishing details include a sign for the side of the van. Make it out of ⅛in ply, paint the sign and then glue it in place. This is easier than painting directly on to the finished van. The sign on my van may not be very original but perhaps you can come up with something better.

Number plates are just pieces of ½ × ½in wood glued on. Use your child's initials or your own car's number to give it a personal touch.

16 Finally fit the axles and wheels on, and the van is ready for its first round of deliveries.

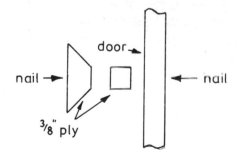

fig 8 Wooden handle for the rear door

Wild West Fort (page 31); Mississippi Riverboat (page 46); Cowboy Town (page 37); Cowboys, Indians and Cavalry (page 42)

GARAGE

(shown in colour on page 17)

This toy is like a dream come true to the parents of children who break everything they touch. It is virtually indestructible — unless set on fire.

1 Take an 8ft length of ½in birch ply, 8in wide. As all the pieces are 8in wide, this is all the wood required except a small extra piece of timber for the ramp.

2 From this 8in-wide strip, cut out the back (24in) and the front (19in), a side (8in), the roof (23in) and the two ramp sides (16in and 8in). By overlapping the ramps as shown in fig 5 you will be able to cut all these pieces from the 8ft length with enough left over for the petrol pump base.

3 Take the garage front (fig 1) and mark and cut out the doorways and windows (see Introduction, Windows).

4 Glue and nail the front to the end wall.

5 Now take the roof/parking area section and glue it into position 2in below the top edge.

6 Attach the rear wall in the same way as the end wall.

7 To build the ramp, first of all glue and nail the inner ramp side to the garage front. Then attach the outer ramp side which makes up the long end wall of the garage.

8 The ramp itself is the only part which may cause any difficulty, so take extra care with your marking out and you will not come to grief. Thicker timber will make the job easier. First cut a strip of wood to the correct width for the ramp, then saw or file the end 'a', as marked on the ramp detail drawing, to the correct angle. Hold this in place and cut off the excess at 'b' (fig 4).

9 Make each petrol pump out of 2 pieces

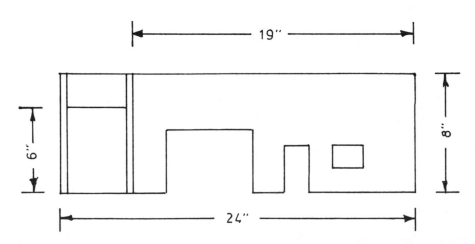

fig 1 Front of garage with lefthand end marked ready to fit ramp

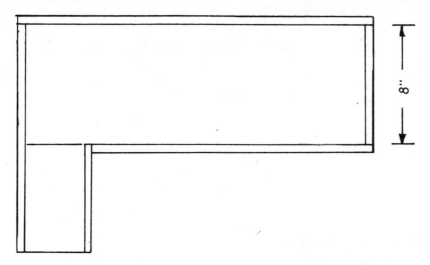

fig 2 Plan of roof/parking area also showing how sides of garage all fit together

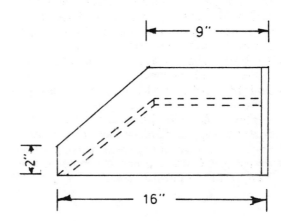

fig 3 View of the outer ramp side, with dotted line indicating position of ramp and roof/parking area

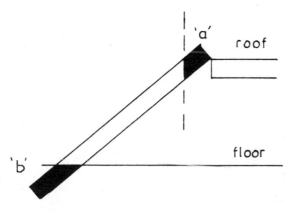

fig 4 Detail of ramp: saw or file away the shaded corners to ensure a smooth join with the roof and floor

21

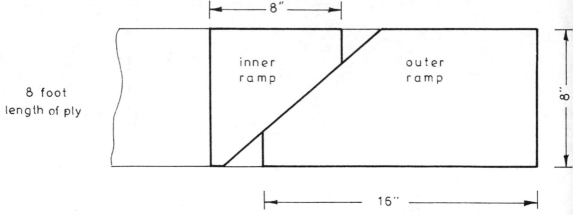

8″

8 foot
length of ply

inner
ramp

outer
ramp

8″

16″

fig 5 Position of ramps to eliminate waste

of ½in ply, 2½ × 1¾in, stuck together. Nail and glue the pumps to the base using two nails for each pump. Nail right through the 8 × 3in base.

10 Paint the garage in your favourite colours and decorate it with stickers bought from a model shop or advertisements taken from magazines etc.

The garage may be mounted on a hardboard base, but children like to try rolling their cars into the garage through the doorways from a great distance and a base tends to hamper this.

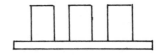

fig 6 Petrol pumps on a base

CAR TRANSPORTER

(shown in colour on page 17)

Although I live in the country, surrounded by farms, just a few miles away there is a large car factory and everytime I drive along the road I see at least three or four trucks delivering cars. My three-year-old daughter is fascinated by them. The one I bought her, made of metal, was soon broken so I decided to make one that would withstand the rigours of children's games.

The drawings and instructions are all for a transporter made out of ½in ply. I made mine out of an old back door but never again. By the time I was half way through I wished I had used ply instead. This vehicle can be made in three sections: the lower deck, the upper deck and the truck.

Lower Deck

1 Cut out the sections for the lower deck. The deck slopes away at the rear so the edges of the two floor sections need to be chamfered to give the correct angle. Make the gaps down the centre as if they were windows (see Introduction, Windows).

2 Cut out the sides and fit ½ × ½in strips of wood to the inside bottom edge to give extra support to the deck. Note that the sides are 1¾in longer than the deck for the ramp hinge.

3 Cut out a piece of wood 5 × 6½in for the ramp. Cut away the bottom corner to give a smooth run on to the road and round off the hinged end (fig 2). This type of hinge attaches the ramp to the deck by means of a dowel hinge, like the castle draw-bridge on page 61. Drill a ¼in hole in both sides of the ramp and both sides of the lower deck as the drawing shows. A short piece of wooden dowelling glued in position provides a good hinge but, for a change, I use pieces of ¼in steel axle with a spring-loaded hub-cap at one end and a spot of super glue on the other end to hold it firm in the ramp.

An alternative is to take two round-headed screws with a ⅝in unthreaded shank. Hold the ramp in position, mark where the corresponding holes in the sides will be and then drill them. The holes should be ⁵⁄₁₆in to give a little clearance for a smooth action.

4 Join the sides to the deck, adding the front section to prevent the cars from rolling off.

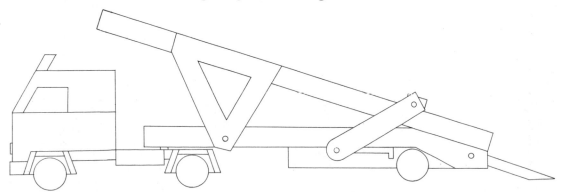

fig 1 Side view of the complete vehicle in the loading position

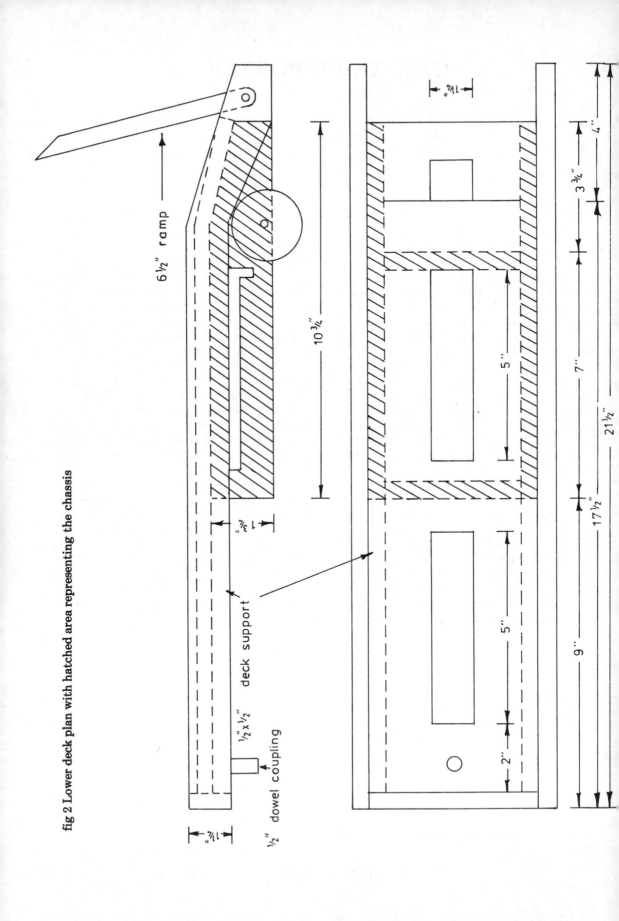

fig 2 Lower deck plan with hatched area representing the chassis

6½" ramp

10¾"

1¾"

½" x ½"
deck support

½" dowel coupling

1¾"

1¾"

5"

5"

2"

4"

3¾"

7"

21½"

17½"

9"

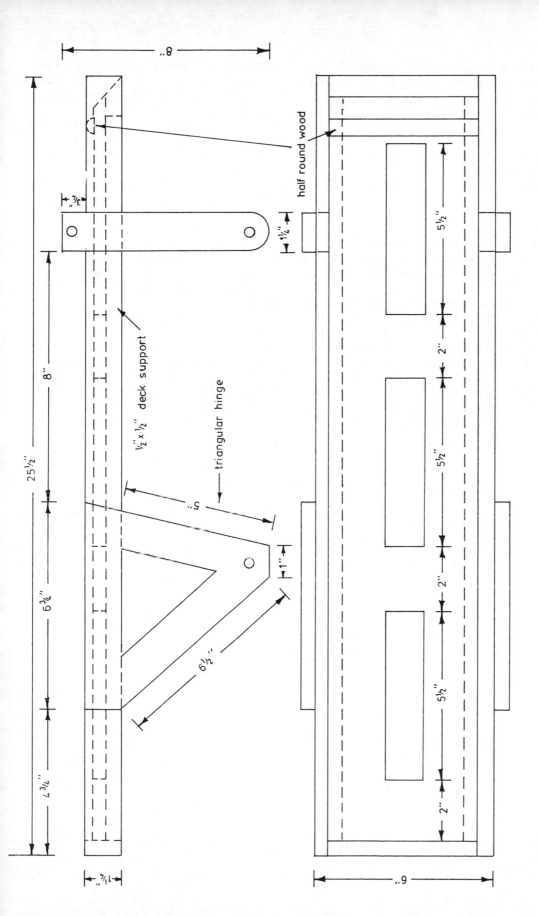

half round wood

$\frac{1}{2}'' \times \frac{1}{2}''$ deck support

triangular hinge

8''

$\frac{3}{8}''$

$1\frac{1}{2}''$

25½''

8''

6¾''

7 ¾''

5''

1''

6½''

$1\frac{1}{2}''$

6''

5½''

2''

5½''

2''

5½''

2''

fig 3 Upper deck

5 Cut out the chassis, indicated by the hatched areas in the diagram, noting that a slot must be cut for the ¼in steel axle joining the bracing supports on either side. Attach it to the underside of the deck.

6 Drill a ½in hole in the underside of the deck and insert a short length of ½in dowelling to act as a simple coupling hook.

Upper Deck

1 Cut out the deck section and the sides. Fit them together and add on the ½ × ½in strip of supporting wood following the plan in fig 3.

2 Cut out two strips of wood to make the triangular-shaped hinges. Make the hinges using any of the methods suggested for the ramp. It is important to ensure that these hinges are fitted in the correct position, so mark where the hinges need to be for the upper and lower decks to meet neatly when in the loading position (fig 1), then attach them.

3 Place a strip of ½in half-round timber or a ½in dowel split in half lengthways across the end. This will prevent the cars from rolling off the back.

4 Add rear bracing supports and, once again, use the spring-loaded hub-caps and steel axles to attach them to the upper deck. A single length of axle the full width of the lower deck, plus the bracing pieces attaches the supports to the lower deck. Make sure they work before attaching them permanently.

This completes the trailer. Hook the ramp forwards to prevent the cars from rolling off the lower deck. The upper deck holds the ramp in position until it is needed.

Truck

1 Cut out the chassis of the truck (fig 4) and be sure to make it the same height as the trailer chassis or it will not couple properly. The height will be determined by the position of the axles. The rear 1¼in section of the chassis slopes down

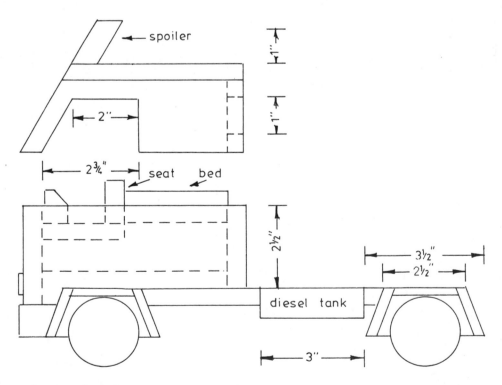

fig 4 Side view of truck

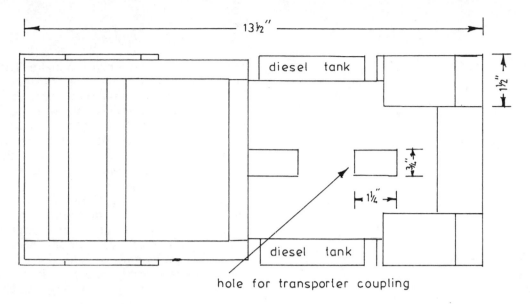

hole for transporter coupling

fig 5 Overhead view of truck

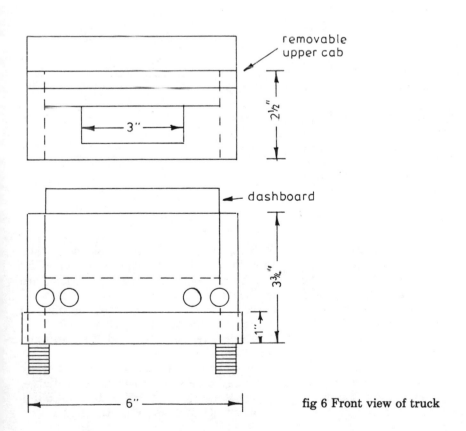

fig 6 Front view of truck

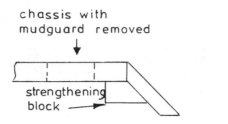

chassis with
mudguard removed

strengthening
block

fig 7 Detail of chassis with mudguard removed

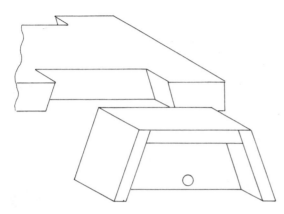

fig 8 Detail of mudguard showing the dovetail joint

between the back wheels. Add a block underneath to give strength to the join (fig 7).

2 Make four mudguards separately (fig 8). Cut a dovetail-type section, the same shape as the mudguard, out of the chassis and glue and nail the mudguards in place. Make diesel tanks out of either 1in dowel or 1 × 1in wood and attach them to the chassis.

3 Make the cab in two parts so that the upper part can be removed and small figures inserted. The drivers can rest in the bed section at the rear of the cab when they are tired. The bed at the back of the cab and the dashboard at the front hold the upper cab section in place. Add on a spoiler and small section of dowelling for the headlights.

4 Finally, fix on the wheels. Use steel axles with spring-loaded hub-caps and 2in ready-made wheels for the truck and the trailer. Varnish the decks and paint the rest of the trailer.

Cars
(shown in colour on page 17)

These cars are very simple to make. They had to be because I made the transporter in November and completely forgot about the cars until Christmas Eve, so it was a mad panic to finish them for Christmas morning. After one false start on an unsuitable design, I settled for this typically European one. I omitted seats for ease of painting and, so far, I haven't received any complaints from the children. If you do decide to add seats, I suggest that you paint the interior before you add the roof. Making the cars is extremely quick and the majority of the time is spent waiting for the paint to dry. Fortunately I used quick-drying paint!

1 Using ¼in ply, cut out the two sides of the car, seeing fig 1 for design and make the windows (see Introduction, Windows). Also make up inner wheel arches following the diagram (fig 9) and glue them in place.

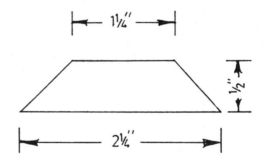

fig 9 Inner wheel arch detail

2 Cut a long section of ply 3in wide. The roof, floor, axles and other parts can all be cut from this, thus ensuring that all are exactly the same width.

3 From this strip cut out the floor and the axles and glue them together.

4 Fit on the car sides and then add the roof bonnet and boot.

5 Make the headlights and the bumpers from any scrap wood you have available. Alternatively, it is quite fun to paint them on, as with the radiator grill.

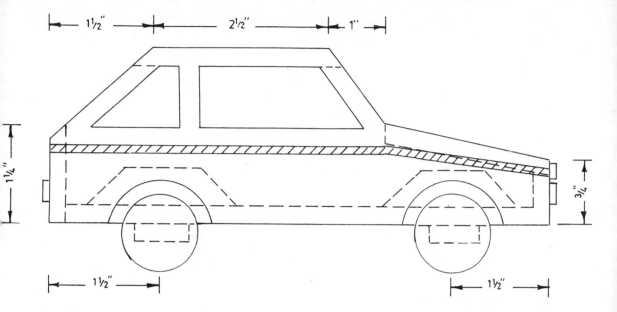

fig 10 Car, with hatched area representing go-fast stripes

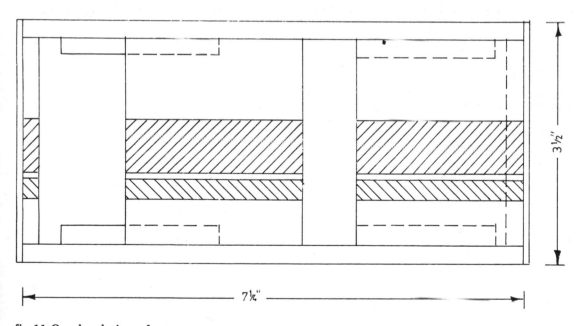

fig 11 Overhead view of car

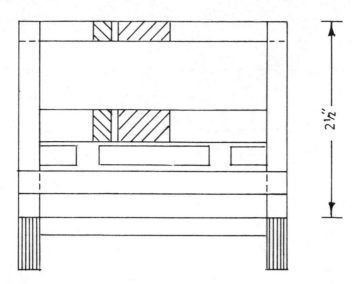

fig 12 Front view of car

6 Paint the car and add the 'go-fast' stripes for decorative effect. Use adhesive tape to give a straight line if your hand is a bit wobbly.

7 The best wheels to use are the 30mm diameter ready-made ones. If you want to make wooden wheels, see page 103 for directions.

8 Attach the wheels using round-headed screws with a long unthreaded shank.

WILD WEST FORT

(shown in colour on page 18)

I had wanted to make a Wild West Fort for a long time, but had been put off by the number of grooves that would have to be cut in order to simulate the logs. As these grooves are the tedious part of this toy, I suggest you practise on a piece of scrap wood before deciding which method to use. A router would have solved all these problems but I was forced to devise other methods.

The easiest way is to cheat and fake the grooves using a magic marker. The added advantage of this is that ¼in ply instead of ⅜in or ½in may be used. I eventually chose to cut V-shaped grooves with a craft knife. Obviously these grooves will weaken the wood so make sure the thickness of the wood is at least ⅜in. I used ½in to be on the safe side, as well as to

give plenty of strength to a toy which will certainly receive lots of rough treatment. Having drawn or cut these grooves, the good news is that the remainder of the toy is easy to make.

1 First of all draw the outline of the fort sides. A back and a front, as in fig 1 and two sides, as in fig 2.
2 Cut out the four sides of the fort and simulate the logs using one of the methods suggested.
3 Fix the 2in ramparts in place by glueing and nailing.
4 Fix the four sides together.
5 Cut out the barracks front and position it. Fix the barracks and then the barracks roof supports in place with nails driven right through the side walls.

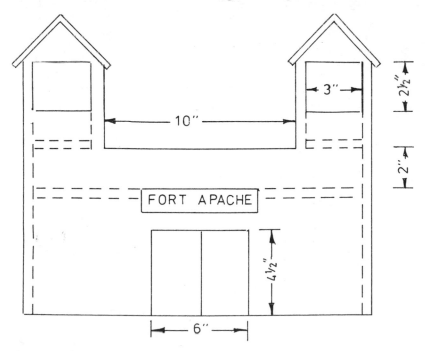

fig 1 Front view of the fort

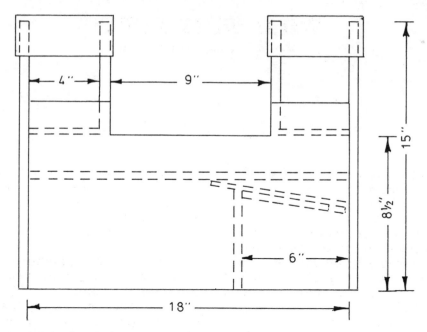

fig 2 Side view of the fort, indicating position
of barracks inside

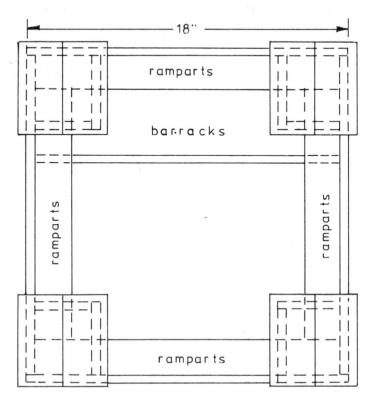

fig 3 Floor plan

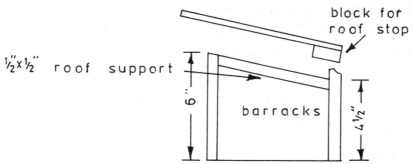

½"×½" roof support

barracks

block for roof stop

6"

4½"

fig 4a Barracks with sliding roof

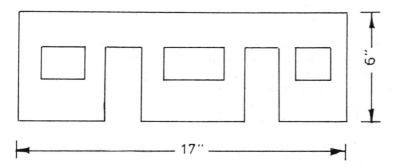

6"

17"

fig 4b Front side of barracks

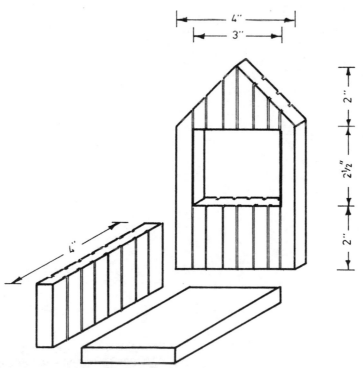

4"

3"

2"

2½"

2"

4"

fig 5 Details of the inner walls and floor of the look-out post

6 Cut out the remaining two inside walls and the floors of each of the four look-out posts illustrated in fig 5. Fix the two walls together, insert the floor and then attach them to the main building. Do the same for each look-out post.

7 Put on the four roofs (see Introduction, Roofs).

8 Make two wooden gates and use strips of piano hinge to fix them in place.

9 The barracks roof is illustrated in fig 4a. A piece of wood fixed to the underside allows the roof to slide forwards, but prevents it from being removed completely. The great advantage of this is that it facilitates access to any part of the fort without disrupting another area which may spoil the game. If you are fitting a base to the fort, remember to insert the barracks roof beforehand as it must be installed from underneath the fort.

10 Finally, glue the Fort Apache sign on to the front of the building and it is ready to repel the Indians, or at least withstand the children.

Straight-sided Ark (page 53); Round-sided Ark (page 52); Zoo and Animals (pages 54 and 58); 3-D Nativity Scene Jigsaw Puzzle (page 82)

COWBOY TOWN

(shown in colour on page 18)

Cowboy towns make excellent toys and the one I had as a boy was my favourite toy for several years. I have incorporated all the features here which I always wanted my own town to have. For extra strength use ½in ply although ⅜in ply would be adequate. Make all the roofs out of ¼in ply and support them with wooden strips fixed to the inside walls of the buildings. It is then easy to remove the roofs by using the windows and doorways as finger holes and just pushing the roofs up from inside. In the line drawings you will see that only the saloon has a back door but obviously one could be added to the other buildings if required.

There are two good methods for hanging doors. Either use conventional hinges and fit them before the sides of the buildings are joined together, or use conventional dressmaker's pins by cutting off the heads and bending two into staple shapes which are then fixed into the doorway opening. Two more pins are bent into 'L' shapes and pushed into the edge of the door as you see in fig 1. The conventional hinges are stronger but the pins

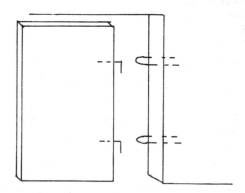

fig 1 Alternative method of hanging doors using straight pins

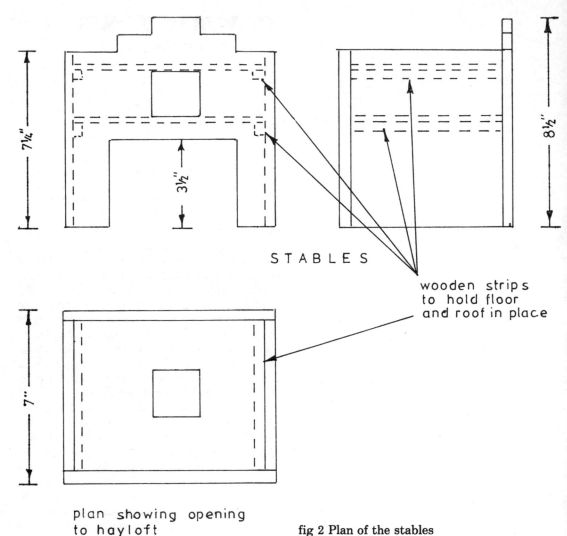

STABLES

wooden strips
to hold floor
and roof in place

plan showing opening
to hayloft

fig 2 Plan of the stables

will prove more economical if you are going to have a lot of doors and they are also easy to repair.

Stable

1 Assemble the stable as illustrated in fig 2 by first cutting out the four sides.
2 Fix wooden strips to two opposite sides to support the hayloft and the roof.
3 Join the four sides together and cut the hayloft floor and the flat roof to size. The stable itself does not need a floor.

Bank/Jail

1 The most convenient place for the jail is right next to the bank, as the robbers can be marched straight from one to the other

— particularly if they are caught red-handed. So, as you see, the bank and jail are built as one. Cut out the four sides of the bank/jail and the floor (figs 3a and 3b).
2 Fix the wooden strips for the roof in position, and attach the veranda roof to the front of the building.
3 Make a partition wall, the same height as the top of the wooden strips, to give extra support to the roof.
4 Join the walls and the floor together and position the supporting $\frac{1}{2} \times \frac{1}{2}$in pillars between the veranda roof and the floor.
5 Make the facia panel with the BANK/JAIL sign on it out of either $\frac{1}{8}$in ply or hardboard and fix it to the veranda roof.

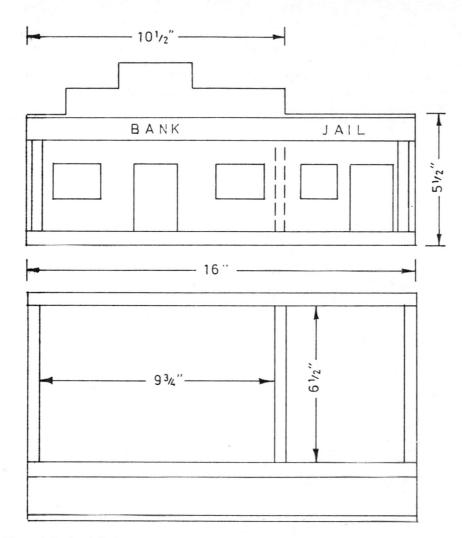

fig 3a Plan of the bank/jail

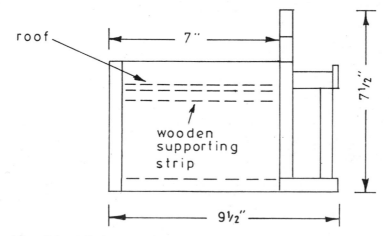

fig 3b Side view of bank/jail showing the
veranda and pillars

Saloon

1 Cut out the four sides and the floor of the saloon.

2 Fix the wooden strips in position to support the floor and roof.

3 Make the external staircase by cutting out two stair shapes from ¼in ply and then fixing the treads and risers in position (fig 7). An alternative simple method is to use five pieces of timber 2 × 2½in laminated on top of each other (fig 7). Attach the staircase to one side of the saloon.

4 Assemble the inside stairs in the same

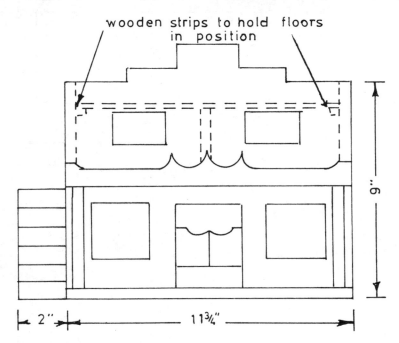

fig 4a Front view of saloon

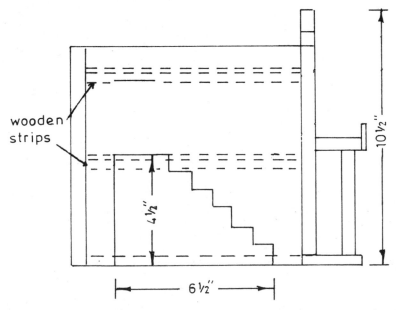

fig 4b Side view of saloon indicating position of exterior staircase

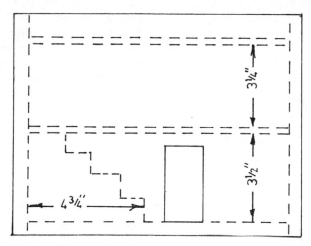

fig 4c Back view of saloon indicating interior staircase

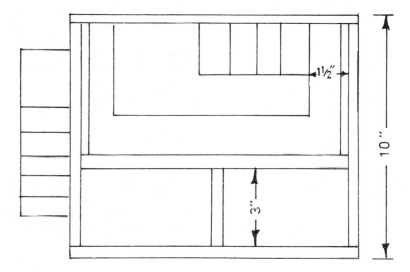

fig 5 Floor plan showing bedrooms and staircases

manner and fix them in place and then attach the veranda roof to the front of the saloon.

5 Join the sides and the ground floor together.

6 Cut the first floor to the correct shape, using ¼in ply, and glue it in place. Then, cut the bedroom walls to the same height as the top of the roof supporting strips and fix them in position.

7 Place ½ × ½in pillars in between the veranda roof and the floor, attach the facia panel and cut the roof to size.

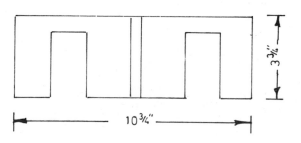

fig 6 Bedroom walls

41

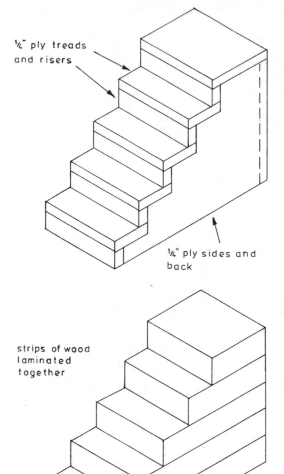

¼" ply treads
and risers

¼" ply sides and
back

strips of wood
laminated
together

fig 7 Two simple methods of constructing
staircases

Horse Trough
Make a simple horse trough by cutting
¼in ply to the sizes indicated in the
diagram. Join them together and
assemble the rails behind from ½ × ½in
wood.

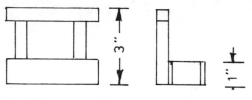

3"

1"

fig 8 Horse trough

Cowboys, Indians and Cavalry
(shown in colour on page 18)

Cut the figures out of ¼in ply following
the outlines in figs 9, 10 and 11. Make as
many as you like and paint them. Details
are easily added, such as a poncho like the
one Clint Eastwood wears. A simple,
alternative method of making cowboys is
by cutting a picture of a cowboy out of a
magazine, glueing it on to a piece of
plywood, cutting around the outline and
fixing it to a base. This saves time spent
painting.

Note that the horses must stand on a
larger base to maintain their balance. The
grids make reproduction simpler and in
each case one square represents a ½ inch.

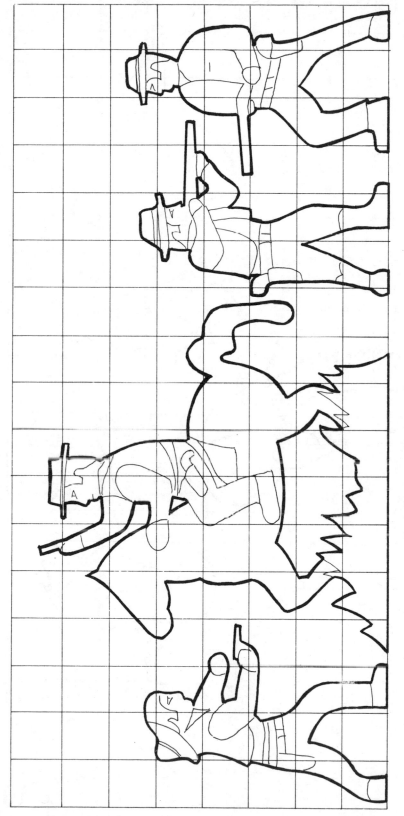

fig 9 Cowboys: each square represents ½in

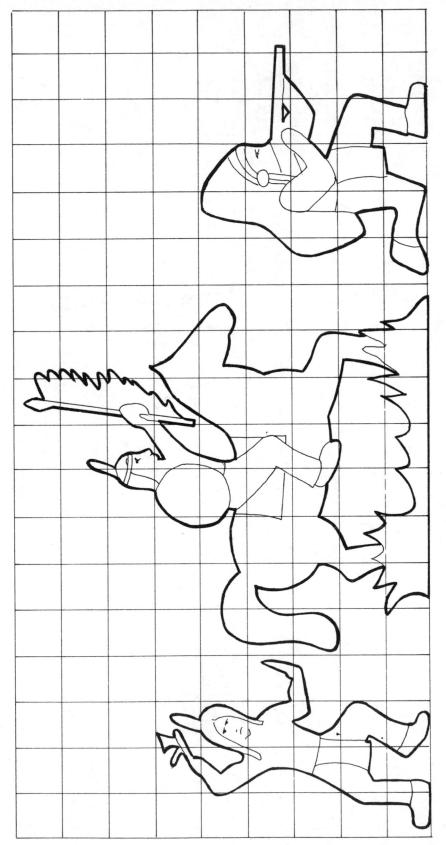

fig 10 Indians: each square represents ½in

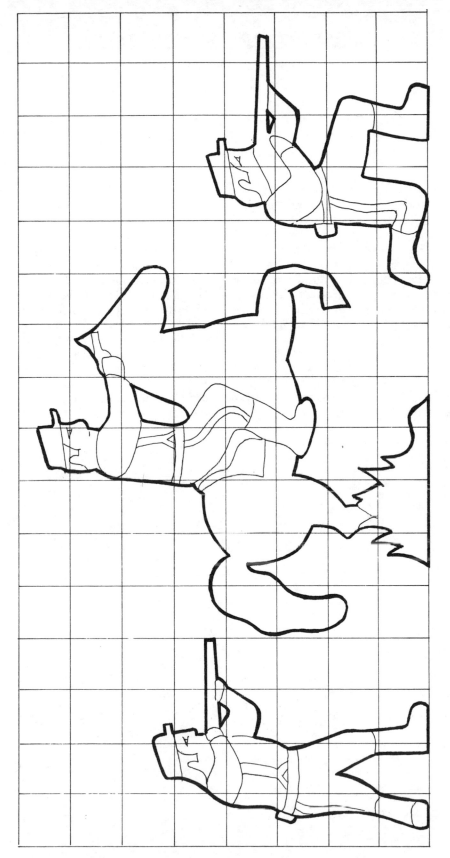

fig 11 Cavalry: each square represents ½in

MISSISSIPPI RIVERBOAT

(shown in colour on page 18)

I have always been attracted to Mississippi riverboats because for me they are the most elegant boats ever built. I started to make a working scale model of one when I was a boy, but had to abandon it when the cost of materials became more than I could afford. It was almost total indulgence that prompted me to make this toy, but fortunately the children seem to enjoy playing with it as much as I enjoyed making it.

This boat has not been made to scale because it is intended as a toy, not as a model, and it is not based on any particular boat, but is merely representative of riverboats in general.

1 Make the hull out of two pieces of ½in ply glued and nailed together, following fig 2 for the size (9¾ × 22½in) and hull shape. If the boat is to float in a paddling-pool, hollow out the upper ring of the hull to give it some buoyancy (see fig 3). Don't forget to cut away a 5¾ × 2¼in section in the stern for the paddle-wheel.

2 Make the decks and the handrails next, as the waste from the inside of the handrails is used for the cabins and the bridge. Cut two pieces of ¼in ply, 10¾ × 22in, for each deck; one of these will become the handrail.

3 Temporarily nail the deck section to the handrail section and mark out the posi-

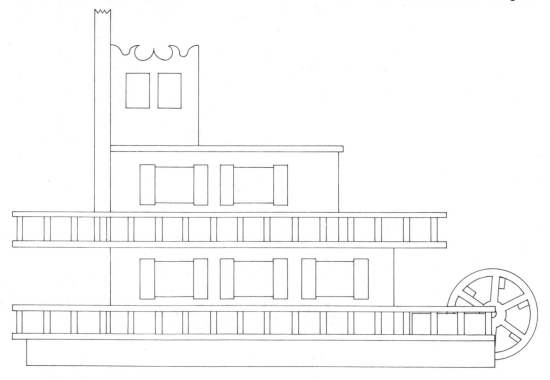

fig 1 Side view of the riverboat

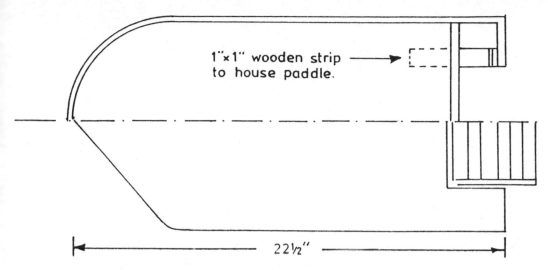

1"×1" wooden strip → to house paddle.

22½"

fig 2 Overhead view of the hull and lower deck

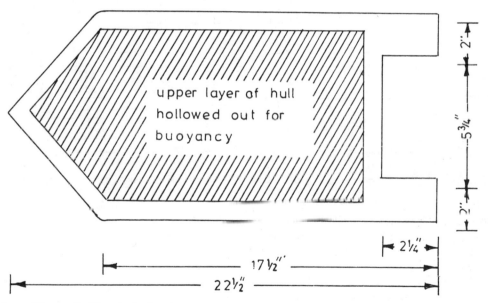

upper layer of hull hollowed out for buoyancy

2"

5¾"

2"

2¼"

17½"

22½"

tion of the railings. Drill ¼in holes for the railings through the deck into the hand-rail section. Avoid drilling straight through the handrail by using a piece of sticking plaster wrapped around the drill bit as a depth gauge.

4 Separate the two pieces of wood and cut out the inside edge of the handrail, making it about ½in wide.

5 Use ¼in dowelling for the railings. Cut it into 1½in lengths and glue them into position.

fig 3 The basic hull shape with the upper layer hollowed out

47

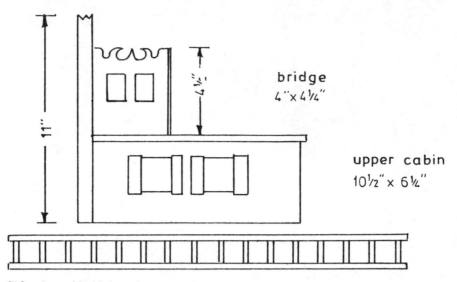

fig 4a Side view of bridge and upper cabin

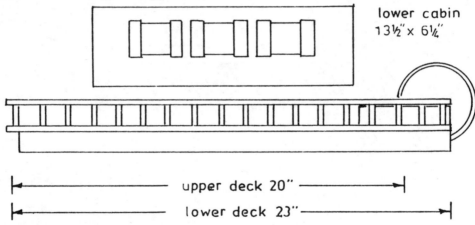

fig 4b Side view of lower cabin

6 Cut out the sides of the cabins and the bridge section illustrated in fig 4 and fix them together. Glue the bridge to the upper cabin.

7 Make shutters out of ¼in ply and glue them either side of the windows.

8 Attach strips of ½ × ½in wood to the decks at the four corners of the cabins to hold them in place during play.

9 Make the two funnels out of ¾in dowelling, 11in long, and cut notches in one end with a fretsaw for the decorative effect. Drill ¼in holes in each funnel for the bracing piece. Make the bracing piece out of ¼in dowel, 5½in long, and glue it into the two holes you have just drilled, as in fig 6. Fix the funnels in position by nailing right through the cabin into them.

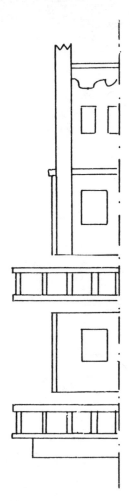

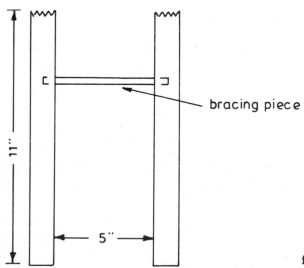

fig 5a Front view

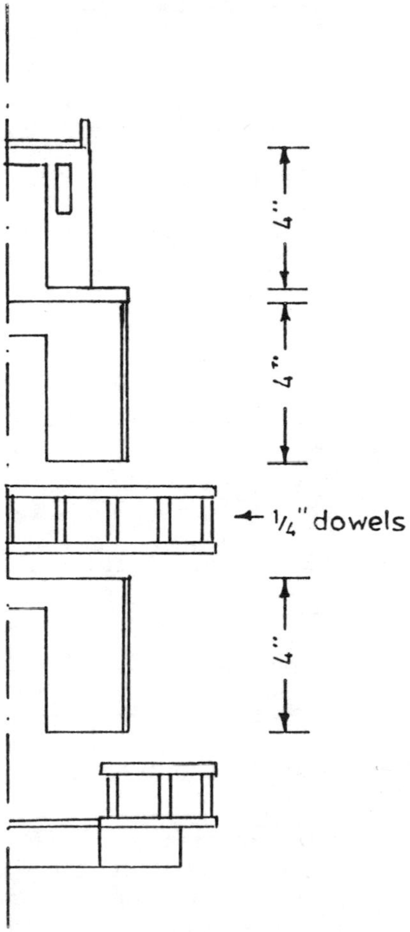

fig 5b Rear view

7"

7"

7"

◄── ¼"dowels

11"

bracing piece

5"

fig 6 Funnel detail

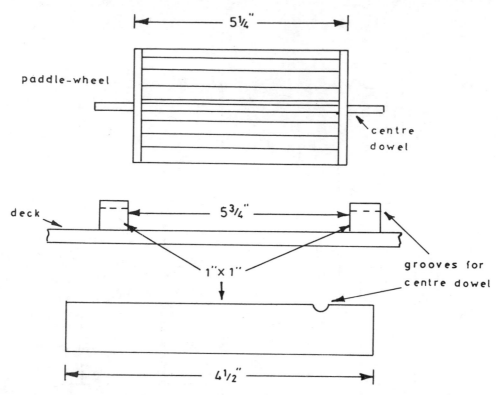

fig 7a Paddle-wheel and its housing

10 Nail two pieces of ¼in ply together and draw the shape of the paddle-wheel on to the top one. This now enables you to cut out both ends at once. Then drill a ¼in hole through both for the centre strip of dowelling. The diameter of the wheels should be 4in.

11 Place one wheel at either end of the dowelling and glue the 5¼in paddles in position. Each paddle will need a ¼in notch in either end so that it will fit on to the wheel, fig 7b.

12 Take two pieces of 1 × 1in wood, cut a semi-circular notch in the top of each and position them either end of the paddle-wheel on the lower deck to support the centre dowel, as shown in figs 2 and 7a. In this way the paddle will spin easily but should it hit any obstruction it will jump out of these small semi-circles rather than break.

13 The riverboat is now ready to be painted.

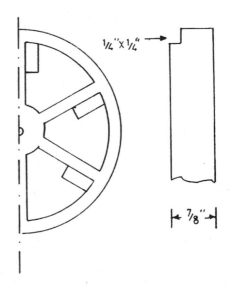

fig 7b Paddle-wheel section showing notches

NOAH'S ARK

(shown in colour on page 35)

Anyone who thinks that there was only one ark is wrong. The fact is that Noah's friends next door, the Jones's, were not going to be outdone so they built an ark as well. Just to add more confusion, the unicorn made it aboard their ark.

The reason for the inclusion of two similar arks is to give a choice depending on your preferences, and the tools and materials you find most convenient to use. If fairly thick ply and an electric drill with a disc sander are available, the best choice is probably the Round-sided Ark. Although fig 1 gives recommended measurements, any thickness of wood

may be used and the ark built to your own requirements.

The House
1 Cut out the four sides of the house, the dimensions for which are illustrated on the Straight-sided Ark (fig 3a and 3c). The same size house will suit both arks.
2 Cut out the square windows as directed in the Introduction, Windows. Make round windows by simply drilling holes with a 1¼in drill bit. Alternatively, these too could be cut with a fretsaw (jigsaw) or hole saw like the square ones.
3 Make shutters out of ¼in ply and glue

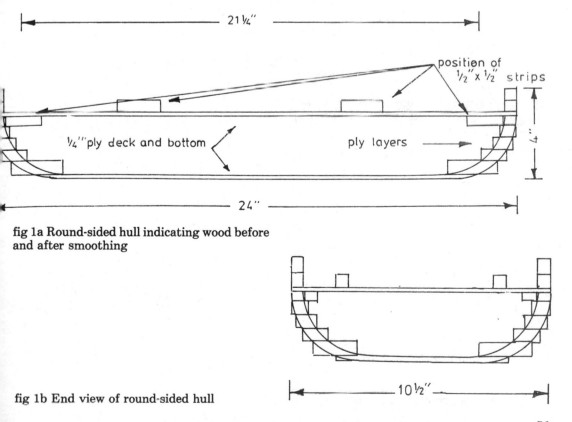

fig 1a Round-sided hull indicating wood before and after smoothing

fig 1b End view of round-sided hull

them in place either side of the windows.
4 Fix the four sides together with glue
and nails and put on the roof (see Introduction, Roofs).

Round-sided Ark
1 To make the hull, cut the required
number of oval rings out of plywood and
laminate them together (fig 2). In order to
reduce the amount of wood wasted, cut
the lower smaller rings out of the internal
waste of the upper rings.
2 Glue and nail two rings together at a
time.
3 Sand the inside until it is smooth and
free from ridges. A final sanding by hand

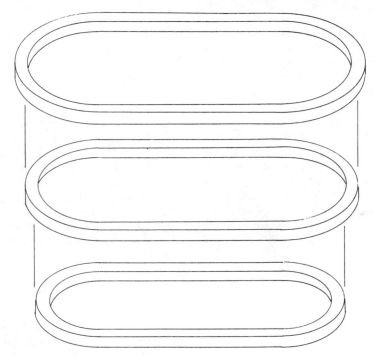

fig 2a Progressively smaller rings of ply
laminated together to make a round-sided hull

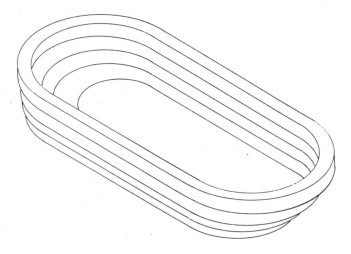

fig 2b Oval rings of round-sided hull

will be required unless the deck is to be permanently fixed.

4 Fix strips of ½ × ½in wood underneath the deck as indicated to hold it in place if the deck is to be a removable one. The advantage of this is that it gives ready access to the hold. Similar blocks on top of the deck will hold the house in position (fig 1). Make the house as instructed on page 51.

5 Sand the outside of the hull and fill in any uneven places on the surface.

6 Paint the ark.

Straight-sided Ark

1 To make the straight-sided hull, cut out the four sides, the bottom and the deck to dimensions shown in fig 3a and 3c.

2 Chamfer them carefully with a file until they fit together perfectly (fig 3b).

3 Glue and nail the sides together except for the front which should be fitted with a magnetic catch at the top and a hinge at the bottom. Add decorative 1in wide stips to either end.

4 Assemble the house and fix blocks on the deck to hold it in position as for the Round-sided Ark, then paint.

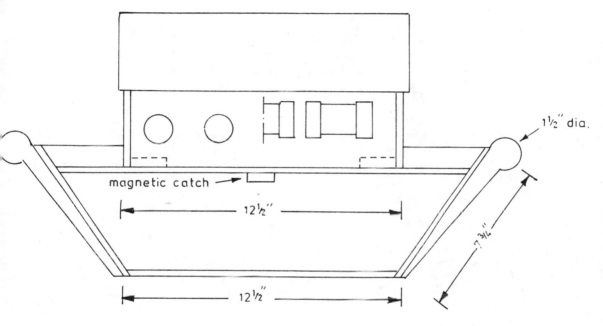

fig 3a Straight-sided hull with house

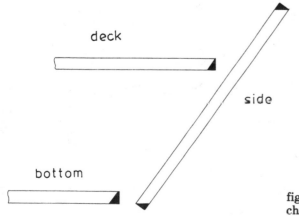

fig 3b The shaded areas indicate sections to be chamfered with a file

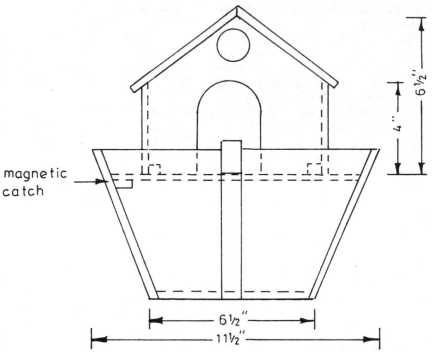

magnetic
catch

fig 3c End view of straight-sided hull and house

Animals and Animal Jigsaw Puzzle
(shown in colour on pages 35 and 88)

Cut the animals out of ⅜in birch ply. This is the ideal thickness because ¼in animals do not stand up satisfactorily, and ½in is too thick for the small animals. Each grid square represents ½in.

fig 4 Heavy lines indicate where to make cuts
from one animal to the next

Jigsaw Puzzle
By carefully positioning the animal shapes close together and cutting them all out of one piece of wood, the 'waste' can form the basis of a fit-in jigsaw puzzle, thus making two toys in one.

Simply trace the animals on to the wood, cut around the outlines and follow lines from one animal to the next. The puzzle should be cut in two or four main sections. When the animals have been cut out, glue the 'waste' to a hardboard base.

ZOO

(shown in colour on page 35)

The animals from Noah's Ark on page 54 may be equally useful as Zoo inhabitants. Choose the child's favourite animals to paint on the Zoo walls.

1 Cut out four principal walls from ¼in ply, following the designs illustrated in fig 1.

2 Make deep notches in either end of each wall, making sure that all the notches are a ¼in wide. Two walls are notched from the top side and two are notched from the bottom side, so as to slot into one another.

3 Apply undercoat throughout and then paint the walls with designs of your choice. Compasses or tins are useful for marking out the round bushes. Pictures of trees, animals and people may be cut from magazines and glued on to the walls.

4 Cut the baseboard out of either hardboard or ¼in ply. The size is not critical,

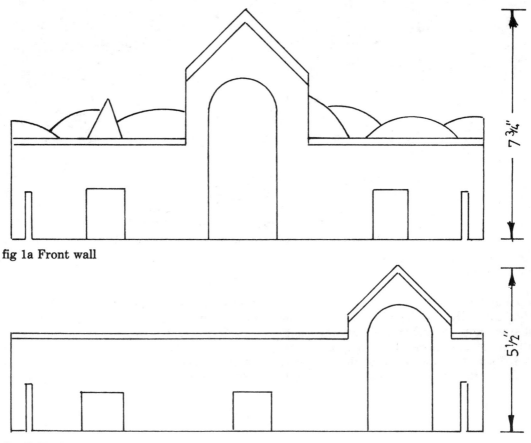

fig 1a Front wall

7 ¾"

fig 1b Back wall

5½"

58

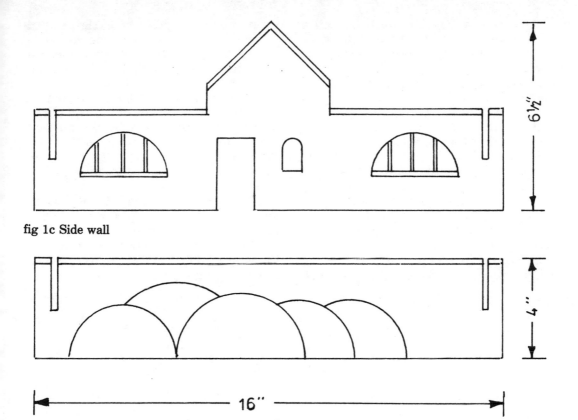

fig 1c Side wall

fig 1d Side wall

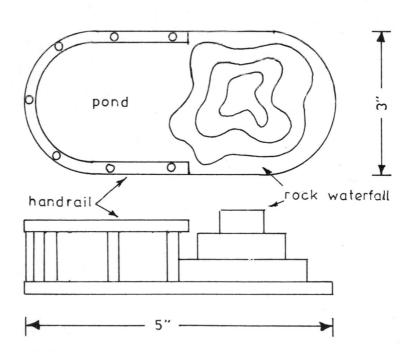

fig 2 Pond and waterfall

as long as it is larger than the zoo area. Undercoat and paint this as well, using masking tape to get crisp lines for the paths.

5 To make the small walls of the internal animal enclosures, cut out strips of wood about 1in high and notch them at either end in exactly the same manner as the zoo walls, so that they slot together.

6 Make the pond by cutting out an oval shape (see fig 2) from ¼in ply. Cut out another piece that is only half the oval to make the handrail. Place the larger piece of wood (the base) over the smaller one (the handrail), use a small nail to hold it temporarily in position and mark the positions of the seven railings.

7 Using a ¼in drill bit, drill right through the base of the pond and into the handrail lying underneath it, taking care not to drill right through it. Wrap a piece of sticking plaster around the drill bit to act as a depth gauge.

8 Separate the two sections, mark and cut out the inside edge of the handrail, making it about ½in wide, and then cut 1¼in lengths of ¼in dowel to form the railings. Glue them into the holes you have drilled in preparation and the handrail is complete.

9 Make a rock waterfall by glueing various shapes of scrap wood on top of one another, gradually making them smaller. Apply undercoat and then paint them, using blues and white to represent the splashing water.

FORT

(shown in colour on page 88)

When I was a boy I had a fort and a cowboy town and the boy next door had a castle. Over a period of time we developed games which evolved into war games, similar to those played by adults.

The soldiers, cowboys, Indians and knights were set out at their battle stations and a coin tossed to decide who should fire first. A length of elastic was used to simulate the shooting. It was fired by holding one end close to the soldier who was doing the firing, then pulling back the elastic, taking aim and releasing it, still holding onto the end by the soldier. An accurate hit knocked over one of the enemy. Only after both sides had fired could moves be made. The elastic was used unstretched to measure out the distance; a longer piece of elastic was used for cavalry moves and cannon fire.

Strict rules of conduct were enforced, any soldier who was hit but did not fall was wounded so a piece of paper representing a bandage was stuck to him and he had to miss a round of firing, after which he was miraculously healed and back in action. Medals and field promotions were awarded for bravery, by means of pen-and-ink marks being drawn on the man in question. Being shot in the back and surviving was treated as cowardice and a firing squad was formed after the battle. Occasionally the bank was robbed in the cowboy town. We usually made a balsa-wood safe and then blew it using a banger — not a good idea to pass on to your children. I only mention it to give an indication of the treatment I expect toys to stand up to. The war games described may increase the play value of these toys.

Painting
There are several good methods for producing the stone-effect finish on castles. The easiest is to use textured paint and add a dye, then only one coat of paint need be applied. An alternative is to apply a texture paint and cover it later with a coat of grey. If textured paint is not available, apply an undercoat and, while it is still wet, cover it with sawdust. When it is dry give it another coat of undercoat and then a top coat. If you are thinking of making two castles for brothers, perhaps a white one and a black one may be a good idea. Use green self-adhesive baize to represent the grassed areas of courtyards and castle grounds.

Drawbridge
The same drawbridge (fig 1) may be used for the fort and the castles although its height depends on which building it is made for. Make it out of ½in ply.
1 Take the two buttress sections and drill a $\frac{5}{16}$in hole in the centre of each inside edge ⅜in above floor level. Do exactly the same on the drawbridge as indicated in fig 1a. Place a short piece of ¼in dowel in the holes on the drawbridge and fit the buttresses on the other end of the dowel.
2 Attach the drawbridge to the main doorway of the castle by nailing right through the castle walls into the buttresses (fig 1b).

Fort
This is a colourful fort, made almost entirely from ¼in birch.

Main Building
1 Cut out the front and the back walls of the main building (fig 2). These are

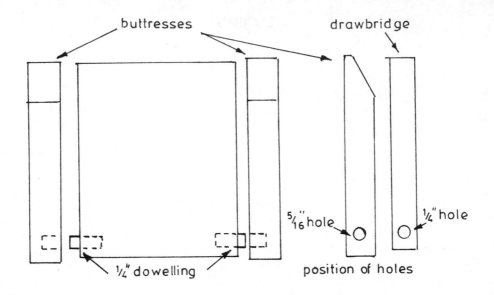

buttresses

drawbridge

$\frac{5}{16}''$ hole

$\frac{1}{4}''$ hole

$\frac{1}{4}''$ dowelling

position of holes

fig 1a Drawbridge

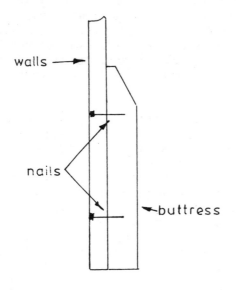

walls

nails

buttress

fig 1b Nail through the wall into the buttresses to secure the drawbridge

identical apart from the doorway in the front.

2 Cut out two sides and the ramparts, ensuring that all are exactly the same width. Make up the framework of the main building, consisting of ramparts and side walls, and then glue and nail the back and front into position.

Gate House

1 Cut out two identical front and back walls, ramparts and the two end pieces (fig 3).

2 Construct a drawbridge and attach it to the front.

3. Join the front and back to the ramparts and walls.

Courtyard and Fort Walls

1 Cut out a base for the entire fort.

2 Place the main building and the gate house on the base.

3 Take 1in wide strips of wood to make the walls, cut them to the required length and join them at the corners with slots, as shown in fig 4b.

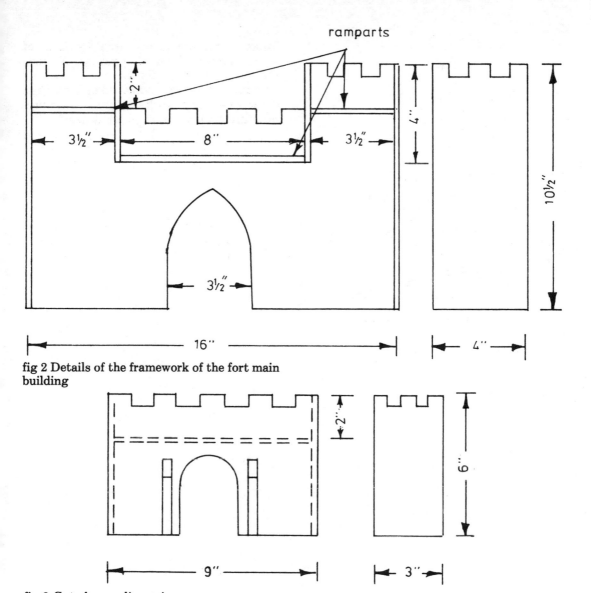

ramparts

fig 2 Details of the framework of the fort main building

fig 3 Gate house dimensions

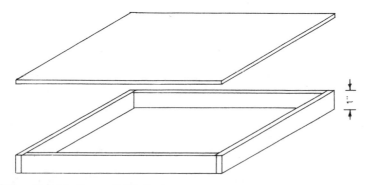

fig 4a Courtyard forming the base of the fort

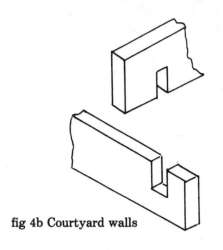

fig 4b Courtyard walls

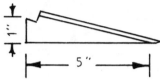

fig 5 Ramp

Ramp
Make a ramp out of three sections of wood glued and nailed together. A cross section is shown in fig 5.

Paint the fort as indicated earlier, then draw the stonework around the main building archway and paint it grey.

TURRETED CASTLE

(shown in colour on page 36)

This castle is tremendously strong provided you use heavy-duty cardboard tubes. It is best if they are at least ½in thick. The diameter is not critical but between 3 and 4in is ideal. It may not always be easy to obtain the tubes, so here are some suggestions for places to try: manufacturers who use textiles which usually come wrapped around suitable tubes; builders' merchants who obtain polythene and other materials in large rolls; carpet shops and, as a last resort, try looking in the phone book for tube manufacturers. Tubes are generally given away free so they are not likely to be over-priced if you do have to buy them. More expensive, but equally good, is plastic rainwater piping.

1 Cut up the tubes into two 18in and two 16in lengths and cut the crenelles for the battlements on one end of each. It may be easiest to use a craft knife for this.

2 Cut 12in slots in the bases of each tube, positioned so that they will fit over the walls and establish the correct castle shape. This can be done with a hacksaw blade or a craft knife.

3 Cut out four circles of wood to the same diameter as the inside of the tubes. Push one about 2in down each tube, and then nail through the side of the tube into the wood. The nailing will be a great deal easier if you use thick wood, such as old floorboards.

4 Cut out three sides, one with a doorway, and fix two 12 × ¼ × ¼in wooden retaining strips to each side. These strips of wood, together with the ramparts, keep the tubes in place when the castle is being played with.

5 Loosely assemble the castle, mark the

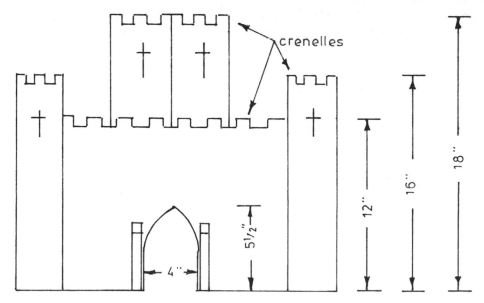

fig 1 Turreted castle dimensions

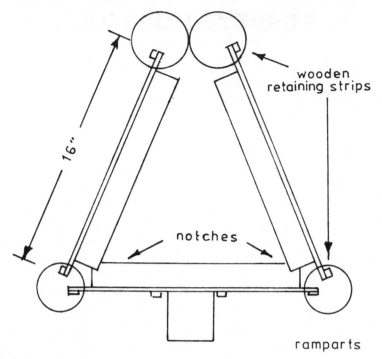

wooden
retaining strips

16"

notches

ramparts

fig 2 Overhead view of castle plan

position where the 12in slots in the two rear larger tubes should be and join the tubes together by knocking nails through one into the other at an angle. Do this at both ends of the tubes — it makes the tubes very difficult to pull apart.

6 Make the ramparts out of three lengths of ½in ply, 2in wide. Assemble the castle and measure the distance between the rear and the front tubes, deduct ½in (¼in at either end) to ensure an easy fit, and then cut the ramparts to that length.

7 Glue and nail the ramparts in place, leaving the front rampart until last as the ends need to be measured and notched to slot in with the side ramparts, to give a closer fit.

8 Build a drawbridge (see page 61), attach it to the main gate and then paint the whole castle.

MEDIEVAL CASTLE

(shown in colour on page 36)

This is a more elaborate castle with stables, a bedroom with a balcony for the damsel in distress, a banqueting hall/guardroom/kitchen, or whatever the child's imagination chooses, and possibly the addition of a simple but effective secret passage.

1 Cut out the outlines of the four sides (figs 1a, 1b, 4a and 4b). Also cut out the removable panel below the balcony and

all the windows and doorways (see Introduction, Windows).

2 Attach thin strips of ply to all four sides at 3¼in from ground level, to act as supports for the floor.

3 Cut out the front and side of the house section of the castle (fig 4c), and the floor (fig 5).

4 At this point of the construction, it helps to assemble the castle loosely to ensure that everything fits (fig 8). Hold

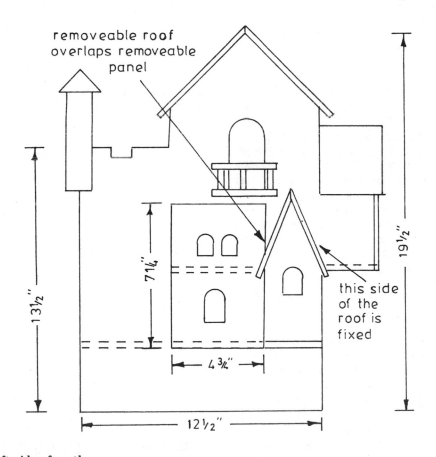

fig 1a Left side of castle

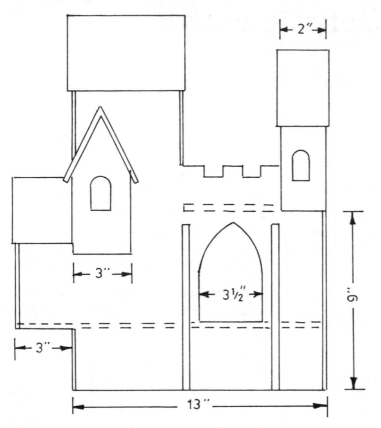

the sections together temporarily with adhesive tape. Once satisfied that everything is in order, remove the tape and build the drawbridge (see page 61). Note that the hinge holes in the buttresses are in a higher position than normal because the drawbridge is raised to floor level. Assemble a ramp (fig 2).

5 Cut the secret door (see fig 7) into one of the outside walls below floor level. Make sure that the edge of the door is bevelled outwards; this allows a tighter fit to be made and prevents the door from being opened outwards.

6 Fit a small hinge to the inside of the door. A gimmick which children seem to like is a small metal latch on the inside which keeps the door bolted until the latch is raised from the outside using a magnet. This makes it virtually undetectable once the doorway is coated with a textured paint, and it is an excellent hiding place for reinforcements, or a small additional present from Father Christmas on Christmas morning which Dad, playing Merlin the Magician, can find by

fig 1b Front of castle showing position of buttresses for drawbridge

Doll's Houses (page 86); detail of interior of Doll's House is shown on page 70.

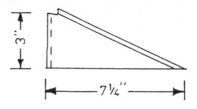

fig 2 Detail of ramp which leads up to the drawbridge

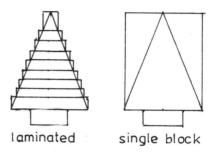

laminated　　　single block

fig 3 Two alternative methods of making spires

opening the secret doorway with the magic key!

7 To make the staircase, mark out two side panels making allowances for the treads and risers to be glued and nailed in position. Then glue and nail the staircase to the side of the house within the courtyard. Alternative staircase details are shown on page 42.

8 For the balcony and the handrail (see fig 9), take two pieces of ¼in ply, lightly nail one on top of the other, mark positions for the railings, and then drill ¼in holes through the balcony section and into, but not through, the handrail.

9 Cut away the inside edge of the handrail, leaving it about ½in wide. Cut ¼in dowelling to 1¾in long and glue in place to make the balcony railings. Fit it outside the bedroom door, after the removable panel has been cut out.

10 Glue and nail the front to the left side of the castle. Then glue and nail the two interior walls of the house together and fix in position. This gives you one corner of the castle.

11 Mark the position of the ramparts and place them around the insides of the walls. Put in the floor and then attach the

1. Interior of Doll's House with Furniture (pages 86 and 99); 2. Deckchair (page 124); 3. Horseshoe Game (page 119); 4. Hoop-la Game (page 119); 5. Picnic Table (page 126); 6. Lace-up Shoe (page 130); 7. Toytown Croquet Game (page 117)

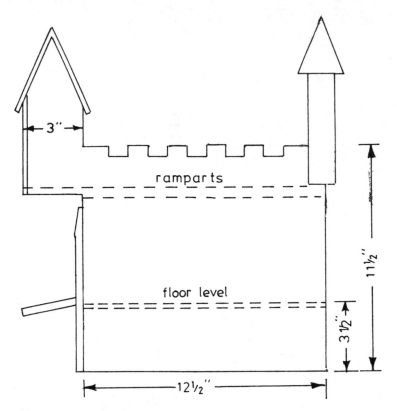

fig 4a Right side of castle

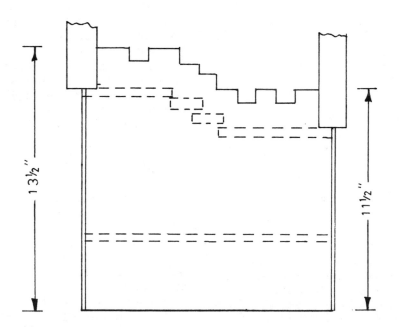

fig 4b Back of castle

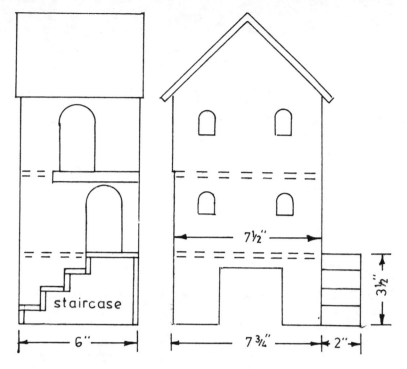

fig 4c Detail of front and side of house section

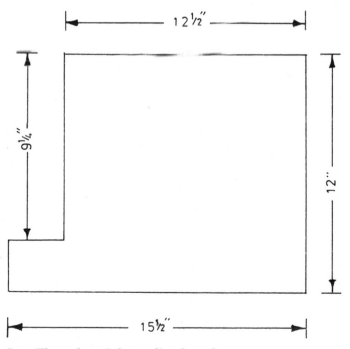

fig 5 Floor plan of the medieval castle

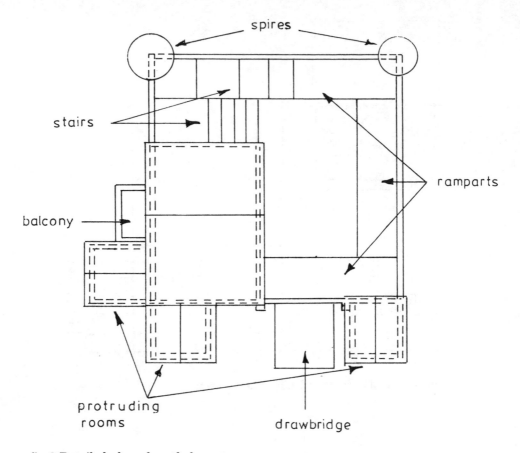

fig 6 Detailed plan of castle layout

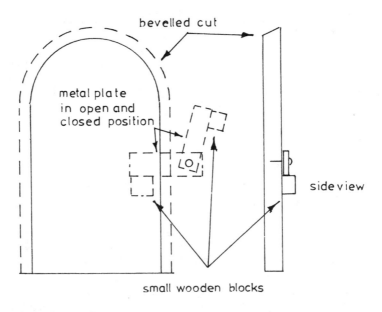

fig 7 Secret doorway

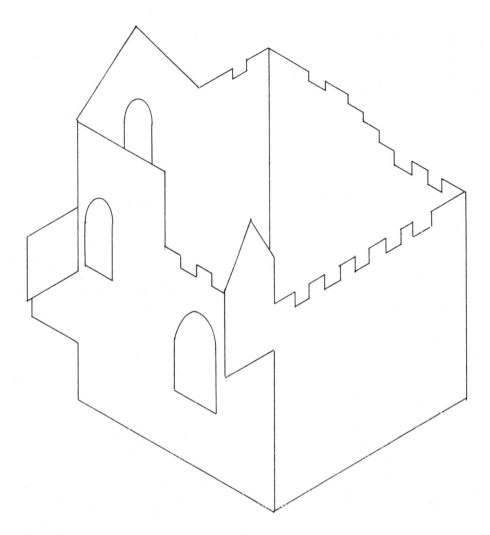

fig 8 Join the four sides temporarily using adhesive tape

remaining two sides of the castle. At last you have something to show for your work.

12 There are three small rooms which are built on to the sides. Cut out the wall sections from ply and attach them to the main building (fig 10).

13 To the top inside edge of the removable panel, glue and nail a piece of ¼in ply, ½in wide (fig 11). Allow half of the width to protrude above the top to act as a stop and prevent the top from coming out accidentally. The panel may be removed by taking off the roof of the small room to the right and pulling the bottom of the panel outwards using the three windows as finger holds. When fixing this roof in position, it is important

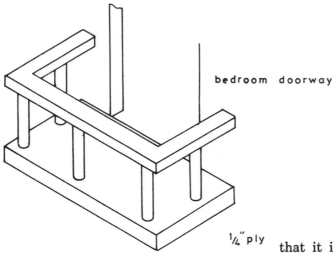

bedroom doorway

¼″ ply

fig 9 Balcony

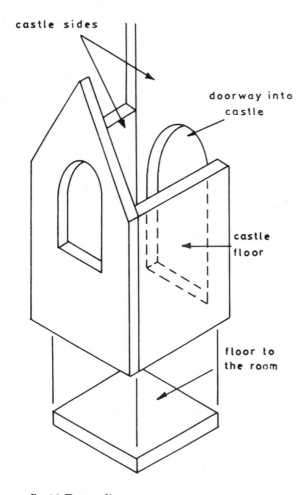

castle sides

doorway into
castle

castle
floor

floor to
the room

fig 10 Protruding room

that it is the lefthand side of the roof which is left loose (see Introduction, Roofs and fig 1a).

14 Perhaps the most daunting part of the castle is the spires, but really they are not too difficult. Make the walls of the towers out of 1½in or 2in plastic water piping. If that is not available, the thicker bottles that bubble bath and other toiletries are sold in will do very nicely.

15 The spires themselves may be made in either of the following ways: make a series of plywood rings of decreasing diameter all laminated together, or cut a single piece of wood as near to a cone shape as possible as seen in fig 3.

16 Cut out a wooden disc the same diameter as the inside of the wall tube. This, when attached to the spire, will hold it in position. Fix a screw through the disc into the bottom of the spiral roof, leaving about 1in of the screw's shank protruding, and cut off the head of the screw. Insert the protruding shank of the screw into an electric drill, wrap a piece of coarse sandpaper around a block of wood, secure the block down and switch on the electric drill. Gently bring the spire into contact with the sandpaper and a smooth finish will soon be obtained. Fill any blemishes with filler and use a finer sandpaper for a perfect finish before painting. The screw may either be left in the wood, removed using a pair of pliers or simply cut or filed off.

17 Fit the spires on the towers and position them on the castle. Put on the roofs and the castle is then ready to paint.

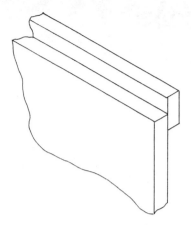

fig 11 Detail of ¼ × ½in strip glued to the top inside edge of the removable panel to hold it in place

Soldiers

I make the soldiers in sets of nine, and in that way they can be used as skittles (fig 12). There is a sergeant who always stands at the back and a soldier with a sad face (inverted mouth), who is always pushed to the front. The smaller size of soldier is drawn to the scale of the fort and castles, but the children prefer to play with the larger ones — so take your pick. Each square represents ¾in for large soldiers or ½in for small soldiers.

Cut all the soldiers out of ¼in birch ply and attach them to a base by glueing and nailing through the base. See the Introduction for painting advice.

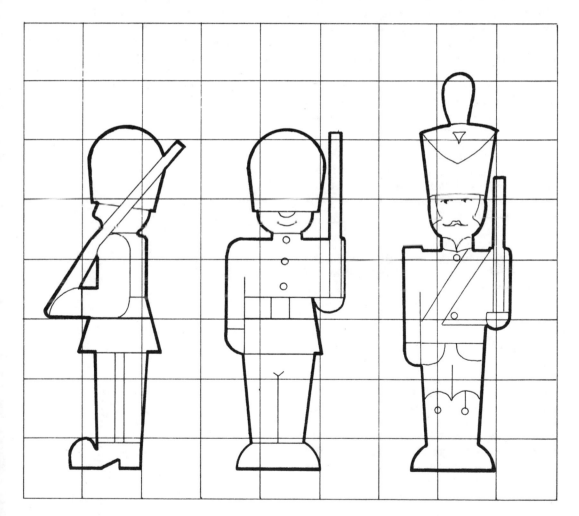

fig 12 Soldiers

3-D JIGSAW PUZZLES

(shown in colour on pages 35 and 36)

These jigsaw puzzles are easy to make provided the fretsaw (jigsaw) is kept perfectly vertical. This is essential if the pieces are to fit together correctly. Try to avoid cutting complicated shapes, as the simpler you make the shape the easier it will be to cut, and your first concern should be that it locks into the surrounding pieces. Both puzzles serve a dual purpose: the Nativity set combines as an attractive Christmas decoration, and the soldiers from the Castle make a wonderful toy on their own.

The puzzles are cut out of ⅜in birch ply. Adhesive tape stuck to the underside of the ply helps to prevent it from splitting as you saw the wood.

Castles and Soldiers
There are three principal sections in this puzzle: the back and front walls of the castle and a strip of soldiers joining the two together.

Castle
1 Draw the outlines of both sides of the castle as in fig 1, and cut them out of the plywood. Don't forget the notches, one in the front wall and one in the back wall of the castle, into which the strip of soldiers slots.
2 Sand down the front of these outlines and apply the undercoat.
3 Transfer the details of the castle on to these outline walls. Draw a sentry in the sentry box, using an outline from fig 2a.
4 Cut out the sentry section first and make sure that the surrounding pieces lock him into the puzzle as demonstrated in fig 3. Then proceed to cut up the castle walls jigsaw-puzzle style in large simple shapes.
5 Remove the adhesive tape and sand the reverse side of the puzzle pieces, put on

the undercoat and draw in the details ready for painting.

Soldiers
1 Draw and then cut out the strip of soldiers, making sure there are slots in either end for the castle walls (fig 2a).
2 Cut around the base of each soldier; they should slot easily into the stand as pieces of the jigsaw puzzle, but the figures themselves remain whole so they may be played with separately.
3 Draw and cut out the cannon (fig 2b).
4 Colour in the walls of the castle and paint the soldiers.

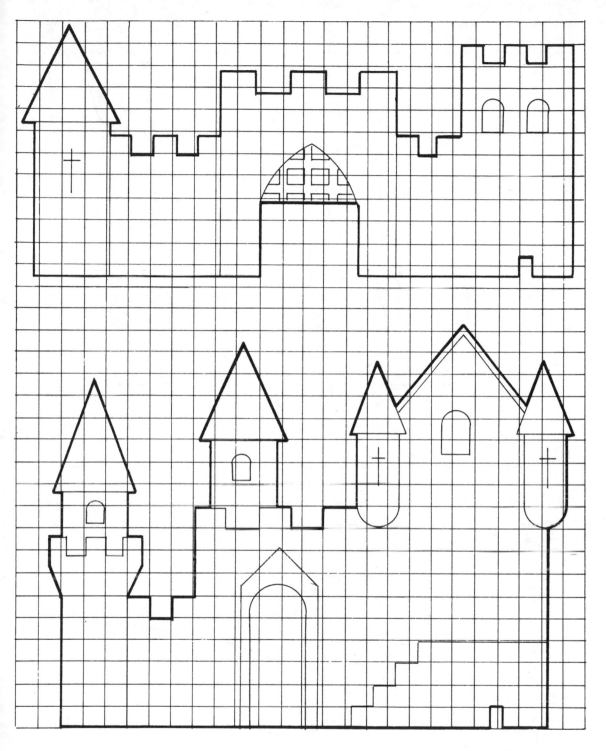

fig 1 Back and front walls of castle: each
square on the grid represents ½in

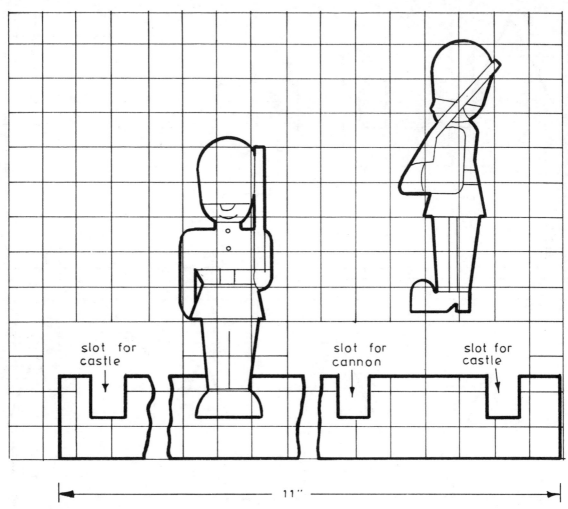

fig 2a Strip of soldiers:each square on the grid
represents ⅜in

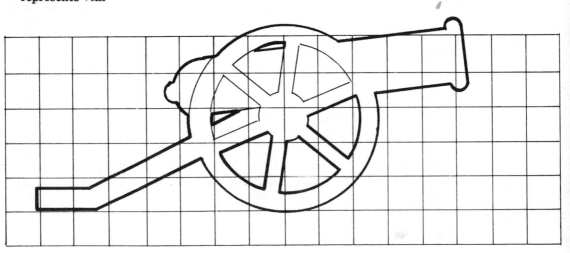

fig 2b Cannon: each square represents ⅜in

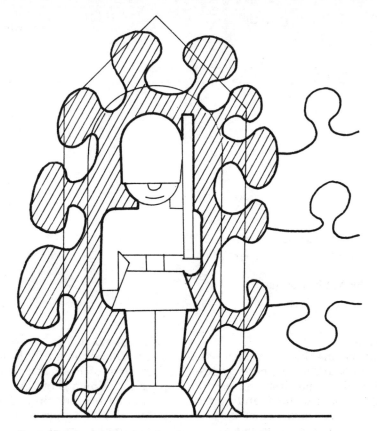

fig 3 Hatched area showing how sentry locks
into jigsaw

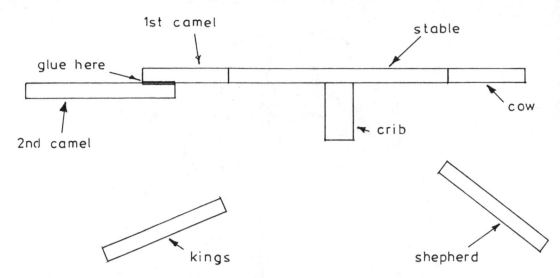

fig 4 Plan of the Nativity scene

Nativity Scene

1 Cut out the outline shapes of the stable, the three kings and the shepherd as seen in fig 5a, b and c. The first and second camel are illustrated in fig 6 and should also be cut out. A third camel may be included if required and likewise an ox.

2 Sand down the front side and draw the remaining figures, apart from the crib, on to the stable.

3 Cut out a crib-shaped slot in the stable wall as this will be the back of the crib. Make one section of the jigsaw out of the whole area surrounding the crib (fig 6). The hatched areas in fig 6 show possible methods of locking the leading camel and the crib into the puzzle and the same applies to the ox.

4 Cut out the remainder of the stable wall in a jigsaw pattern, keeping the shapes simple and not too small.

5 Build the crib by cutting out the pieces for it (fig 5b) and glueing them together.

6 Glue the head of the second camel to the side of the first.

7 Remove the adhesive tape from the reverse side of the jigsaw pieces, sand them down, apply a coat of clear varnish to seal the wood, and leave to dry.

8 Stain all the figures with a wood stain, applying one coat to the lighter areas and two or three to the darker areas. White paint blended into the varnish before it dries will achieve a halo effect. Apply a thin coat of clear varnish to the whole puzzle to finish it off. As several coats of varnish are used, they should be diluted with thinners to prevent an unattractive build-up of varnish.

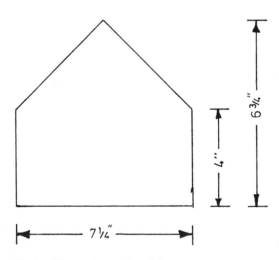

fig 5a Dimensions of stable

fig 5b Nativity figures

fig 5c Nativity figures

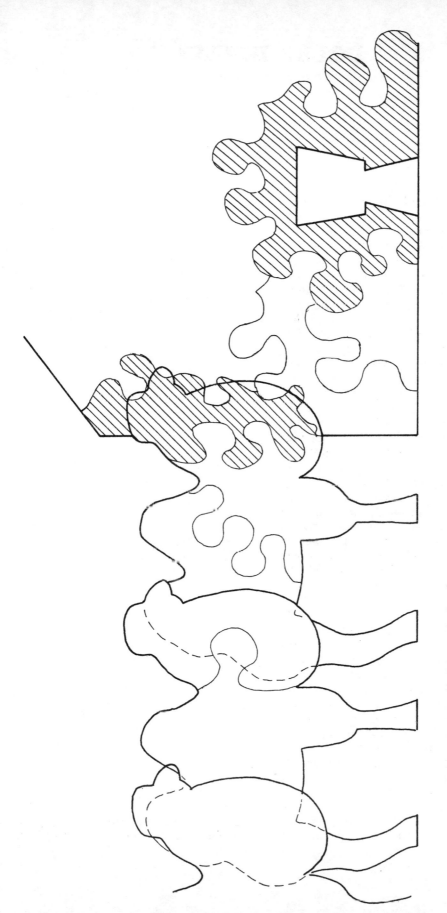

fig 6 Hatched areas are possible methods of locking the leading camel and crib into the puzzle

DOLL'S HOUSES

(shown in colour on page 69)

These houses are built to be played with, not to be kept as models. They are designed to be strong and the inside is left as simple as possible. It is a matter of individual choice as to whether internal doors, architraves, lights and other details are added. Personally I don't think it is necessary. Neither kitchen nor bathroom furniture is included in my designs because I prefer my children not to spend their playtime acting out household chores. Perhaps, more truthfully, sinks and baths look stupid made out of wood. The dining-table and chairs, and the sitting room suite are not to the same scale as the beds and other furniture, because the dolls which are readily available in the shops are not hinged at the waist and consequently fall off chairs if they are made to scale.

Make these Georgian-style doll's houses as simple or as elaborate as you like. Beginning with the basic house, additional items may be included such as stairs, rear door and windows, the working loft ladder, attic windows and the child's initials to be inserted between the date.

Except where otherwise stated, all the material is ¼in birch ply. See fig 1a, b and c for the dimensions of the three alternative houses. The diagrams provide a detailed view of the largest, most elaborate doll's house. Fig 2 however gives the measurements of a four- or six-roomed house and the doors, windows and other fittings may be the same size for all three. Fitting the roof is exactly the same as stated in the Introduction, Roofs. The cornice is a purely decorative addition and is very effective on the roof and front door. Where nailing is not mentioned, glue alone is strong enough and nailing would spoil the appearance.

Railway Station (page 108); Train (page 103); Farm (page 112); Farm Animals (page 114)

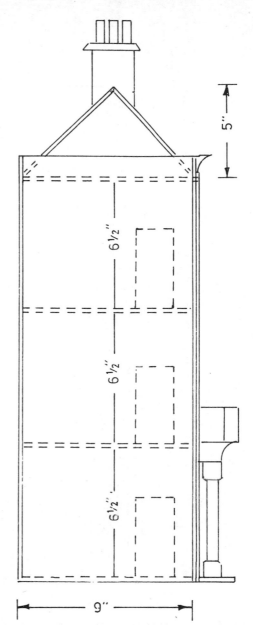

fig 1a Side view of doll's house showing interior divisions of rooms

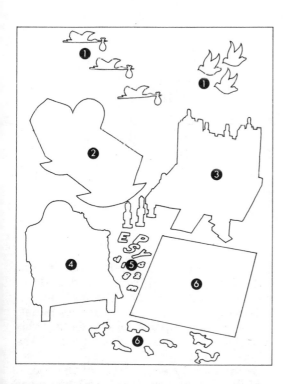

1. Crib Mobile (page 128); 2. Rocking Cradle (page 122); 3. Fort (page 61); 4. Doll's Bed (page 120); 5. Alphabet Letters (page 131); 6. Animals Jigsaw (page 54)

The Front

1 Mark out the front accurately. Always check the measurements before cutting.

2 Cut out each window pane separately (see Introduction, Windows). Some ingenuity is required to cut out all the window panes on the largest house, as the fretsaw (jigsaw) is not large enough to manage it comfortably. It may be done by

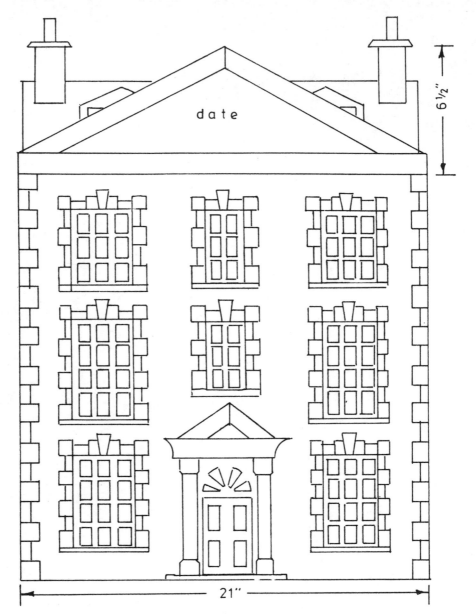

fig 1b Front view of largest doll's house

drilling more than one hole in some of the panes and reversing the blade so that it cuts towards you (fig 3).

An easier method of cutting out these windows is to cut out the complete window $\frac{3}{16}$in larger all around. Then it is a lot simpler to cut out the panes. Stain the frames and then glue the whole window section back into the house front (fig 4). The extra $\frac{3}{16}$in enables the frame to be glued to the stonework which surrounds the window. Birch ply will split when cut thinly, as in these window panes, but adhesive tape stuck to the underside of the panes will eliminate this problem.

Having cut out all the window panes, file and sandpaper them smooth. This completes the most tedious part of the whole project.

3 Sandpaper the entire front of the house.

4 Make the stonework edging around the windows and the whole building out of ¼in birch ply. The mortar joints are simulated by saw or file cuts.

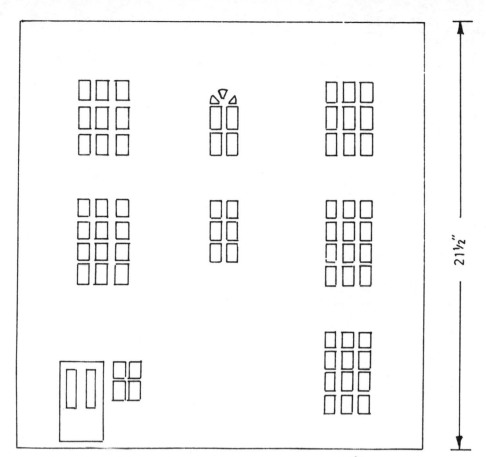

fig 1c Rear view of large doll's house showing how the windows should be positioned symetrically

5 Make the cornice — the decorative triangle on the front of the house — out of wooden picture framing with the rebate removed, or a moulding. Glue it directly to the front of the house. It is important to use a mitre joint at the apex of the cornice. If this is difficult, cut the joint as accurately as possible and then file it down until it is perfect. Cut the moulding to the required length when the mitre is perfect.

6 Cut the date and your child's initials out of ¼in ply as in fig 5 and glue directly on to the front of the house.

7 Make a front door slightly larger than the opening cut out for it. Draw the

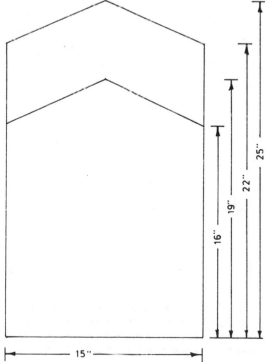

fig 2 Dimensions of the four- and six-roomed houses

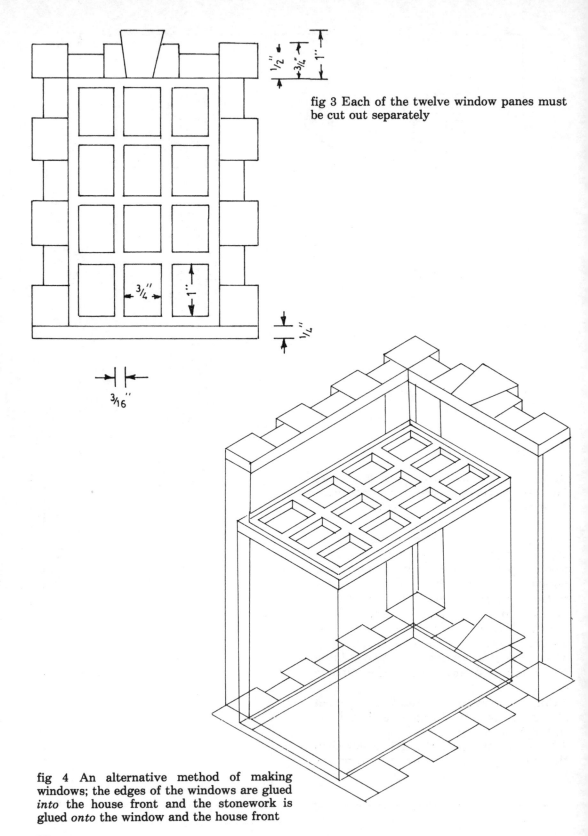

fig 3 Each of the twelve window panes must be cut out separately

fig 4 An alternative method of making windows; the edges of the windows are glued *into* the house front and the stonework is glued *onto* the window and the house front

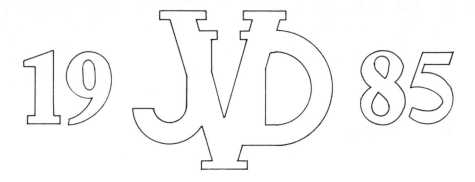

fig 5 Date and child's initials

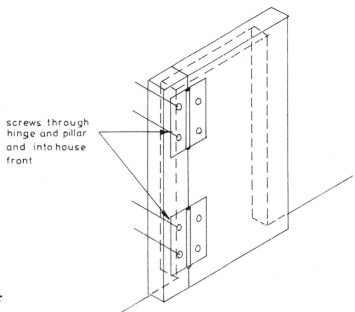

screws through
hinge and pillar
and into house
front

fig 6 Rear view of the front door

panelling on it in pencil. Screw small music-box hinges to the back of the door. Using longer screws, screw right through the hinge and a ½in-wide strip of ¼in ply into the rear of the house front at the edge of the door opening, see fig 6. This enables the door to be opened inwards but not outwards, just like a real door.

8 The portico is illustrated in fig 7. Cut dowels to size for the pillars. Draw around the ¾in dowel on to the 1⅛in dowel, and chamfer it with a file to ¾in. Glue and nail the two together to form the column.

9 Glue and nail the base and the ceiling of the portico in position and put on the triangular facia. Cut the roof of the portico to size and fit it by nailing through the portico into the roof.

10 Fit the cornice in the same manner as in 5, but additional mitres will have to be cut to take the cornice down the side of the portico. This completes the front.

Rooms

Before starting the rooms, read the section on *Stairs*, below.

1 Cut out the walls and the floors. Decide at this point whether or not you are going to include stairs and/or a loft ladder and if so, cut the openings at this stage.

2 Join the internal walls by cutting slots

93

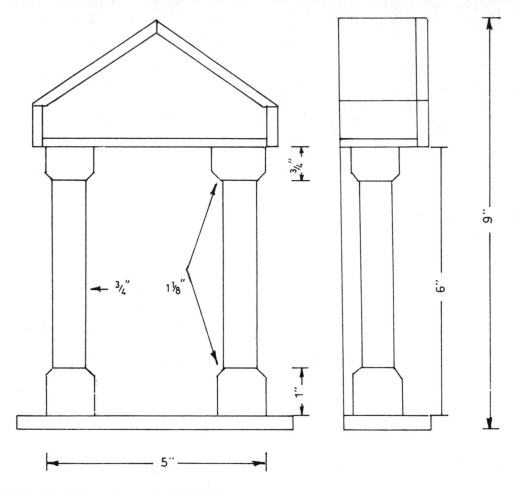

fig 7 Portico, before the cornice is fitted

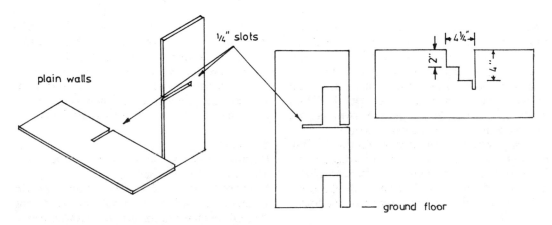

fig 8 Method of joining internal walls and
making openings for stairwells and doorways

94

¼in wide, half the height of the wall as in fig 8. The remaining walls, the ceiling and the floor are glued and nailed in the usual way.

Stairs

The most important point to remember when making the stairs is that they start on one floor and finish on the one above — this may seem obvious but accurate measurements are required if the stairs are not to be left dangling in mid-air. If you are not confident of working this out accurately, make the stairs first, then make the floor to fit the stairs. Minor inaccuracies will not matter.

1 Cut the treads and the risers from a fairly long piece of ply 2in wide. This ensures that all the stairs are the same width.

2 Cut out the stair framework as shown in fig 9a and glue and nail it together. At this point, check that the staircase fits the opening.

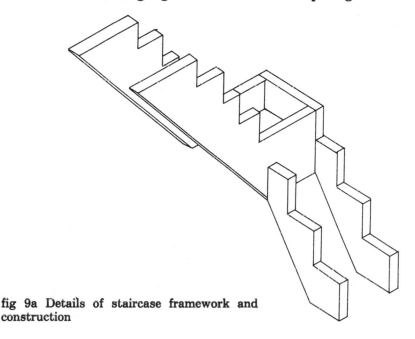

fig 9a Details of staircase framework and construction

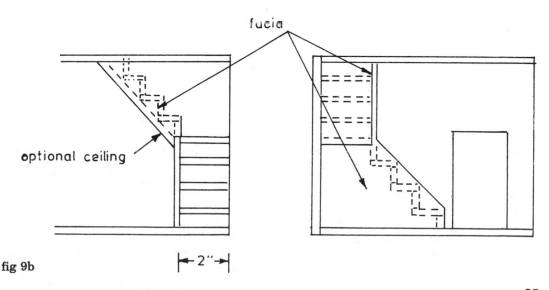

fucia

optional ceiling

fig 9b

|← 2" →|

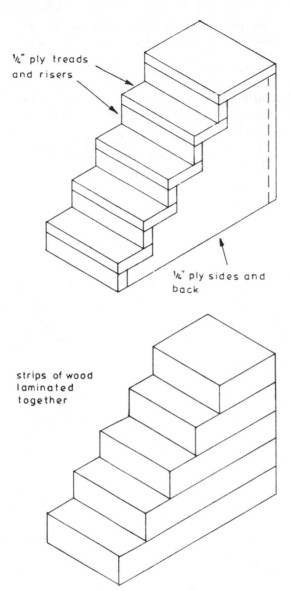

¼" ply treads and risers

¼" ply sides and back

strips of wood laminated together

fig 10 Two simple staircases

3 From now on it is easy. Simply glue the treads and risers in place on the framework as can be seen in 9b.

4 Glue a facia on to the stairs to hide the edges and a strip of ply underneath the stairs as an optional ceiling. This isn't really necessary, but I think it adds a finishing touch. Now glue the stairs in place.

5 Two alternative methods of making simple staircases are shown above. The top example shows treads and risers glued to a framework with a solid base

96

and the lower example is simply strips of wood laminated together to the required height.

Interior Doors
A very simple hinge may be made using pins. Bend two pins into staple shapes and fix them in the doorway opening and bend two more into 'L' shapes and push them into the door (fig 11).

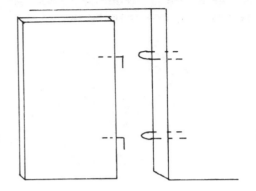

fig 11 A simple door on hinges

Loft Ladder
The ladder is made from $\frac{3}{8} \times \frac{3}{8}$in strips of timber and ¼in dowel (see figs 12a and b).
1 Mark out and drill ¼in holes in the two $\frac{3}{8}$in strips for the rungs to fit into. Take care not to drill straight through the wood. A piece of sticking plaster wrapped around the drill bit will act as a depth gauge.
2 Cut the rungs to size and glue them in place.
3 The width of the loft door is the same as the opening you have cut for it, but the length will be shorter because of the hinge — just how much shorter depends on your placing of the dowelling hinge. Try making it ¼in shorter than the opening and then file it down to make a perfect fit.
4 Take four strips of $\frac{3}{8} \times \frac{3}{8}$in timber, pairs 'a' and 'b' and drill a ¼in diameter hole in each one (fig 12b) — again taking care not to drill right through.
5 Glue and nail pair 'a' on to the loft door. Glue pair 'c' across both.
6 In each of the holes in pair 'a' place a short piece of dowel. Then place pair 'b' on the other end of the dowels. This is the hinge.

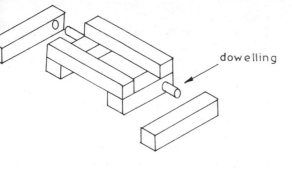

7 Glue pair 'b' to the attic floor, either side of the opening. It produces a hinge effect so that, when the ladder is in place, it holds the door closed until the child pulls it open and the ladder slides down by gravity, just as a real one does.

dowelling

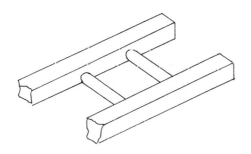

fig 12a Loft ladder

ladder slides freely between the opening assembly

DOWN

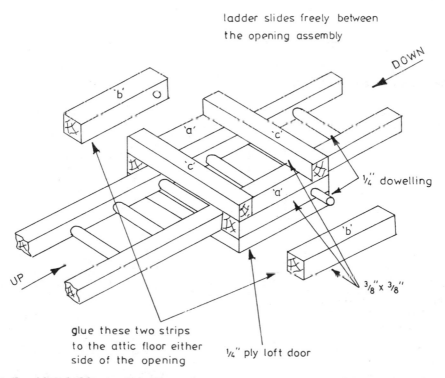

¼" dowelling

UP

'b'

³⁄₈" x ³⁄₈"

glue these two strips to the attic floor either side of the opening

¼" ply loft door

fig 12b Details of loft ladder construction

Attic Windows

1 If attic windows are to be included see fig 13, two holes must be cut in the front slope of the roof before they can be added and before the roof is fixed in position.

2 Cut out the window panes as directed earlier. Cut out sides and glue them to the window frame. Remember that the angle of the rear edge is determined by the pitch of the main roof, and must be chamfered to fit it.

3 Glue the framework together and then glue the whole attic window to the main roof.

Chimneys

1 Use ½in dowelling for the chimney pots, which are fitted by drilling ½in holes in the top section of the stack and glueing in the pots (fig 14a and b).

2 Make the chimney stacks by cutting out four sides, making sure that the pitch of the roof and the angle of the notch in the stack fit one another exactly. Add the top section with the pots attached and glue the chimneys in the most attractive position.

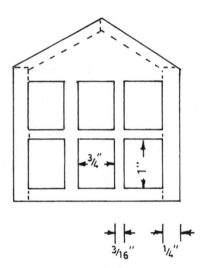

fig 13a Attic window: front view

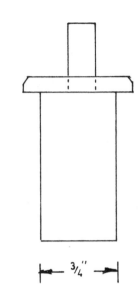

fig 14a Chimney: front view

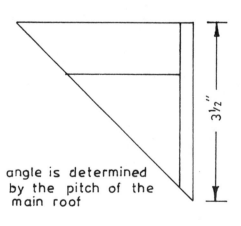

fig 13b Attic window: side view

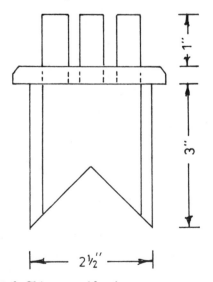

fig 14b Chimney: side view

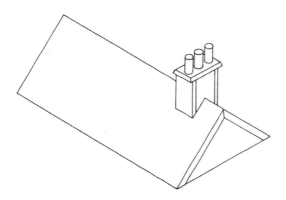

fig 14c Overhead view of chimney fitted on roof

The house is now ready to be varnished. I use silk sheen varnish, allowing about six coats and rubbing down between each coat.

The front of the doll's house is free-standing as the porch holds it in an upright position, which means that there are no hinges for boisterous children to swing on and break. If you wish, a magnetic catch can be fitted to secure the front of the house.

The back of the house is either left plain, or doors and windows are added as shown in fig 1c, and then glued and nailed in place. Difficulties should not be encountered even on the large house, as the back is a few inches shorter than the front, which makes all the difference when manoeuvring the fretsaw (jigsaw).

Furniture
(shown in colour on pages 17 and 70)

There is sufficient furniture illustrated here to fill even the large house. I have not used any nails or panel pins when making the furniture, but have relied on the glue alone. The occasional leg has been broken off a bed when it has been stood on or run over by a go-kart, but even then it is the wood which has snapped rather than the joint — a worthy testimonial for the strength of the glue. Only the dining chairs and the double bed require any drilling, and that is for the dowelling which represents the legs and the spindle backs. The covers for the settees and armchairs can be glued in place, but no doubt anyone with any sort of skill with needle and cotton will be able to improve on this.

ARMCHAIR

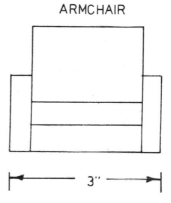

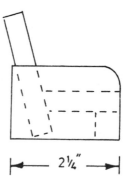

fig 15a Doll's house furniture

SETTEE

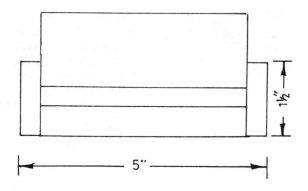

SINGLE BED

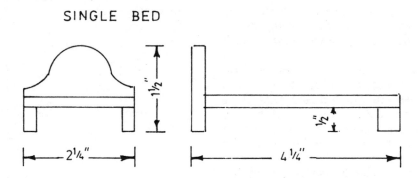

CHAIR

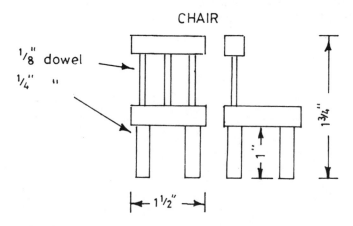

fig 15b Doll's house furniture

BUNK BEDS
and
LADDER

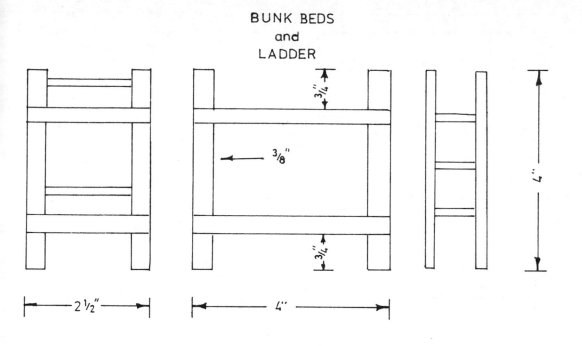

$\frac{3}{4}$"

$\frac{3}{8}$"

$\frac{3}{4}$"

4"

2 $\frac{1}{2}$"

4"

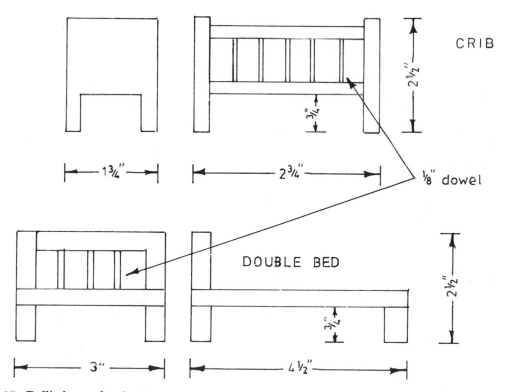

CRIB

2 $\frac{1}{2}$"

$\frac{3}{4}$"

1 $\frac{3}{4}$"

2 $\frac{3}{4}$"

$\frac{1}{8}$" dowel

DOUBLE BED

2 $\frac{1}{2}$"

$\frac{3}{4}$"

3"

4 $\frac{1}{2}$"

fig 15c Doll's house furniture

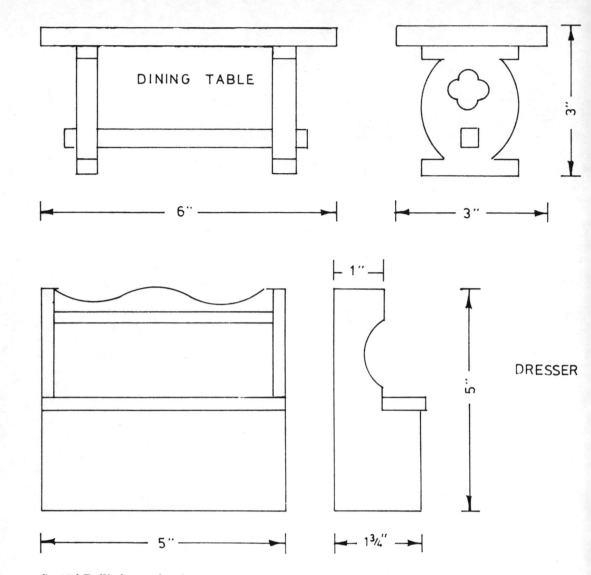

DINING TABLE

6"

3"

3"

1"

5"

DRESSER

5"

1¾"

fig 15d Doll's house furniture

TRAIN

(shown in colour on page 87)

This may well be a passenger train but that doesn't prevent animals, dolls, ornaments, money boxes and plenty of other things from hitching a ride. The detachable roof on the carriage is well worth the extra trouble.

Wheels

There are rather a lot of wheels so I like to get them out of the way first. Use either of these methods.

METHOD A

1 Draw a circle of the required diameter on to a piece of ⅜in ply. Cut it out with a fretsaw (jigsaw).
2 Drill a ¼in hole in the centre for the axle.
3 Put four of these wheels on to a ¼in bolt and tighten it up with a nut and washer.
4 Insert the threaded end of the bolt in a drill and turn the wheels against a piece of sandpaper. This will smooth away all the irregularities and the wheels should be perfectly round. By doing four wheels

at once you can be certain that all the wheels on one part of the train are exactly the same size. Keep the wheels in separate groups until they are needed.

METHOD B

1 Use a hole saw to cut out the wheels. A hole saw consists of a drill bit with a cylindrical saw blade attached to it (see

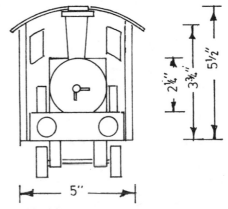

fig 1b Engine front view with dimensions

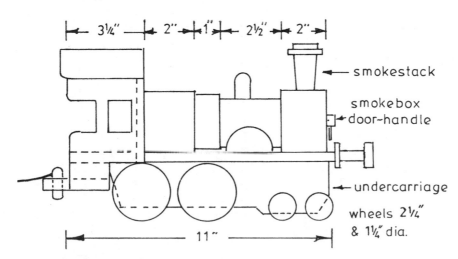

smokestack

smokebox door-handle

undercarriage

wheels 2¼" & 1¼" dia.

fig 1a Engine side view with dimensions

103

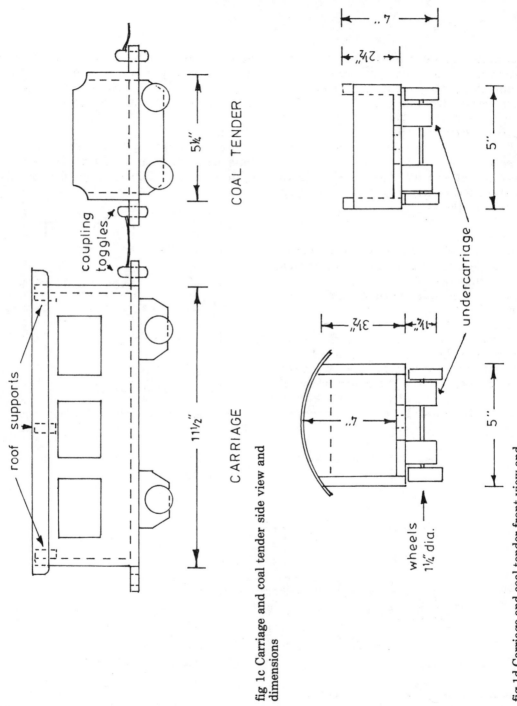

COAL TENDER

CARRIAGE

coupling toggles

roof supports

5¼"

11½"

fig 1c Carriage and coal tender side view and dimensions

7"

2½"

3½"

1¼"

7"

5"

5"

undercarriage

wheels 1¼" dia.

fig 1d Carriage and coal tender front view and dimensions

Introduction, Tools). Select the diameter of blade you require and another blade two sizes smaller.

2 Fit the hole saw with the smaller blade into your electric drill and using ⅜in ply, drill a hole about ⅛in deep with the saw blade. This is for a decorative finish. As you do this you will automatically be making a ¼in hole for the axle with the drill bit.

3 Change the blade for the larger one, line up the drill bit with the axle hole and cut right through the ply with the blade. You have now made one perfect wheel. It is obviously easier if you make all the decorative cuts first and then change the blade and cut out the wheels all at once.

Engine

1 Make the boiler in exactly the same way as the wheels. The drawing (fig 2) shows how the sections fit together with a dowel running through the centre hole of the rings to align them.

2 Attach the square section of the engine, made out of ⅜in ply, to the boiler and fix it to the floor. See plan in fig 1a and b.

3 To make the smokestack, take a piece of 1in dowelling and taper it down to ¾in. Do this by securing a screw in the top of the dowel and cutting the head off the screw, placing the screw and dowel in a drill and spinning it against sandpaper until you have finished the taper.

4 Remove the screw and cover the hole with a larger piece of dowel or a disc cut from ply. Cover this with a final piece of 1in dowel. Alternatively you could make a straight-sided smokestack from ¾in dowelling.

5 Drill two ¾in holes in the top of the boiler and insert the two pieces of dowelling for the smokestack and the dome. Insert a piece of ¼in dowel with two ⅛in dowels attached in the hole at the front of the boiler to make the smokebox door handle.

6 Cut out the undercarriage of the engine

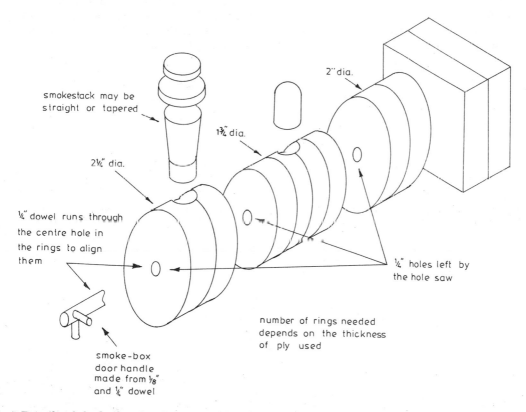

smokestack may be straight or tapered

2″ dia.

1¾″ dia.

2¼″ dia.

¼″ dowel runs through the centre hole in the rings to align them

¼″ holes left by the hole saw

number of rings needed depends on the thickness of ply used

smoke-box door handle made from ⅛″ and ¼″ dowel

fig 2 Details of the boiler showing assembly of ring sections (fig 3) and drill holes in it for the axles, making sure that the bottoms of the wheels will all be level.

7 Fix bracing pieces between the two sides of the undercarriage and attach them to the floor of the engine.

8 Cut out the cab sections of the engine from ⅜in ply and join them together.

9 Cut the roof to size out of ⅛in ply and soak it in hot water. It can then be bent into the shape of the curve of the cab. Glue and nail it in place.

10 Cut out two semi-circular sections and fix them either side of the boiler and make the buffers from pieces of dowelling and attach them to the front.

11 Fix a piece of ⅜in ply between the cab sides on a level with the floor of the tender. The connecting eyes are made in this as shown in fig 4a.

12 Paint the engine before attaching the wheels and place steel washers on the axles between the undercarriage and the wheels to make the train run better.

Coal Tender

1 Cut out the four sides and the floor of the tender following the dimensions in fig

1c and d.

2 Drill a hole in either end of the floor section to make a connecting eye (fig 4b). Make it slightly larger than the size of the dowel you intend to use as a coupling toggle to connect the train together.

3 Cut out the undercarriage from either ¾in wood or two pieces of ⅜in ply glued together. Drill holes for the axles in it and attach the wheels.

Carriage

1 Cut out the four sides and the floor and make the windows (fig 1c and d, and see Introduction, Windows).

2 Cut out and attach the undercarriage to the floor. Note that there are four sections of undercarriage.

3 Cut three roof support sections out of ⅜in ply and make sure that they all follow the curve of the roof framework. By fitting the roof to the support sections instead of to the carriage itself, the roof is removable.

4 Cut a roof out of ⅛in ply and soak it, in exactly the same way as the roof to the engine cab. Bend it into shape and attach it with glue and nails.

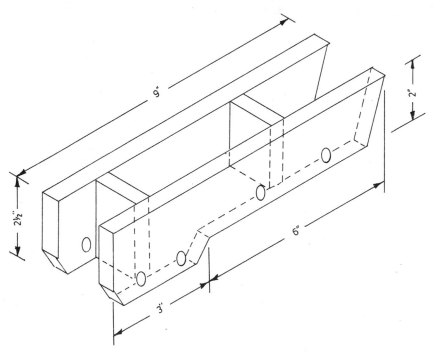

fig 3 Engine undercarriage with bracing pieces

106

fig 4b Detail of connecting eye

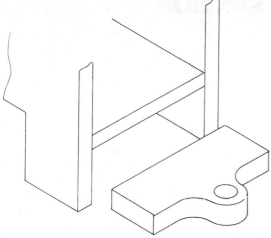

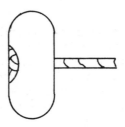

fig 4a The section with the connecting eye of the engine fits beneath the cab floor.

fig 4c Coupling toggle

5 Join the train together by making coupling toggles (fig 4b and c) out of pieces of dowelling and drilling a hole through each one. Countersink the holes on one side for the knot.

RAILWAY STATION

(shown in colour on page 87)

When you have made the train, why not make this station for it to stop at? It is a very simple design and intended as a toy rather than a model. The length of the platform is not stated because you can choose whatever length is suitable. It can also be made either in sections or in one long piece, depending on which is easier for you to store. An advantage of making it in short lengths is that you are more likely to be able to use up any scrap wood.

1 For the main station building use ¼in ply to cut out two gable ends and the back and front walls using the dimensions in fig 1a and b.

2 Make the windows and doorway (see Introduction, Windows).

3 Fix two strips of wood to the inside of the gable ends to act as roof supports, as shown in the detailed drawing in fig 4.

4 Join the front and back sections to the gable ends and then put the roof on (see Introduction, Roofs) and a chimney as described for the Farm, page 112.

5 Make a signboard, using ½ × ½in wood for the posts and a board long enough to carry the name you choose. Fit the posts into a base to make it freestanding.

6 Make the platform by cutting strips of ply 1in wide for the base (fig 2). Join them together as shown and make as many sections as you need, depending on the length required, then add on the platform itself.

7 Make the signal box (fig 3) by cutting out the four sides. Draw on the windows and the doors and then cut them out. Either keep the windows straightforward, like those on the main building, or make them a little bit more complex as illustrated here. To make the smaller, more complicated ones, nail the two sides of the building together and then cut both out at once. Do the same with the two ends but remember that a doorway takes the place

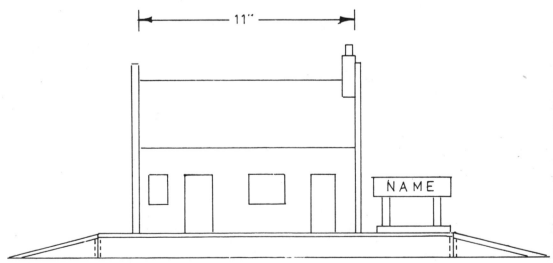

fig 1a Station building and platform with signboard

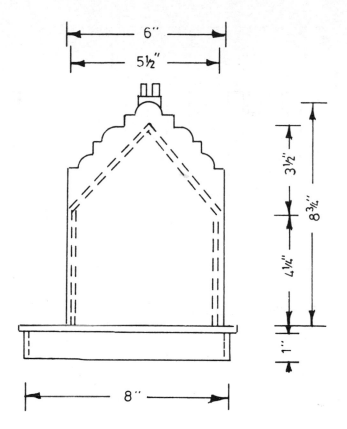

fig 1b End view of station building with
decorative gables

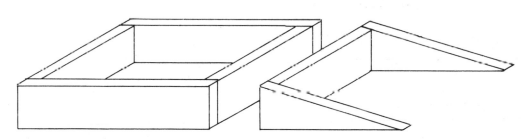

fig 2 Detail of platform base

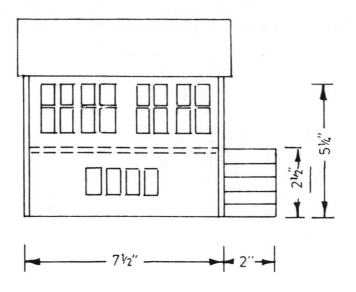

fig 3a Side view of signal box

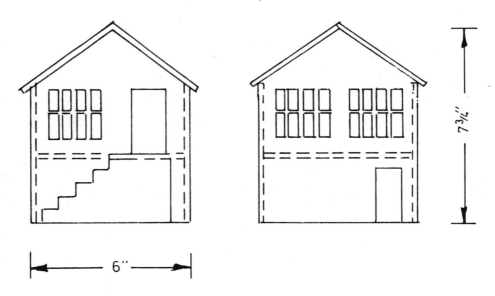

fig 3b End view of signal box showing stair-case

fig 3c Opposite end of signal box with windows

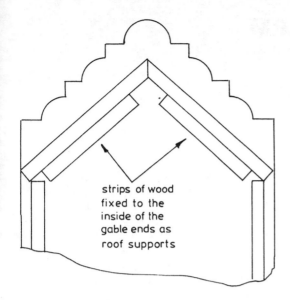

strips of wood
fixed to the
inside of the
gable ends as
roof supports

fig 4 Detail of the station roof

of one of the windows. This method saves some time marking out the wood and time spent undoing the blades on the fretsaw (jigsaw) to insert it through the windows.
8 Cut out a piece of ¼in ply for the floor and attach it at either side. Make sure that the bottom of the doorway is flush with the top of the floor and then glue it at back and front.
9 Put the roof on as directed in the Introduction, Roofs.
10 There are two easy methods for making the staircase. Both of these, outlined on page 42 for the Cowboy Town saloon, are excellent.

FARM

(shown in colour on page 87)

This toy is extremely popular with both boys and girls. The basic layout can easily be extended by making more stables or barns and buying additional animals and farm machinery.

1 Cut out all the pieces from ¼in ply to the sizes shown in the line drawings (fig 1a, b, c and d). The construction of the buildings is extremely straightforward, so simply look in the Introduction for Windows, Roofs and Painting. For the chimney simply take a small block of wood with a 'V' shaped groove cut in it. Drill two holes in the top for the chimney pot dowel. Glue onto the roof top.

2 Place the farm buildings on a baseboard with a fence (fig 2). The size of the baseboard and the length of the fence depend on how large a farm it is.

3 Make the pond out of a piece of ¼in ply, cut to any shape or size you like. Paint the edge the same colour as the baseboard, make the grass surround out of self-adhesive green baize and paint the water blue (fig 3).

4 Any left-over baize may also be used to create a grass meadow, possibly with a stream running through it to the pond, and perhaps a bridge over the stream for the farmer and his cattle. The possibilities are endless and for this reason I leave it to you to decide how big to make the baseboard.

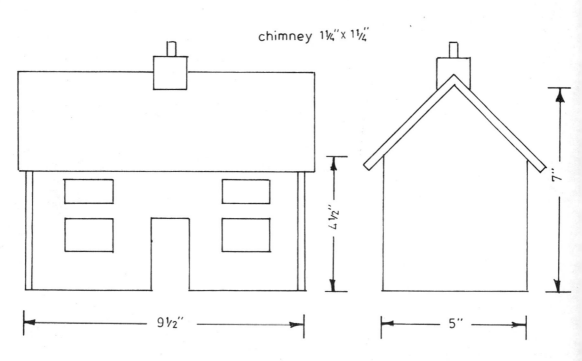

chimney 1¼" x 1¼"

7"

4½"

9½"

5"

fig 1a Farmhouse

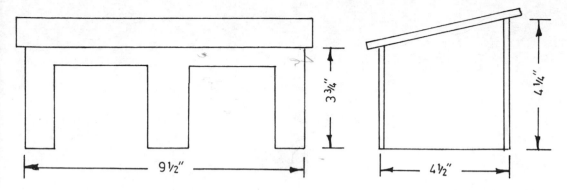

fig 1b Stable with sloping roof

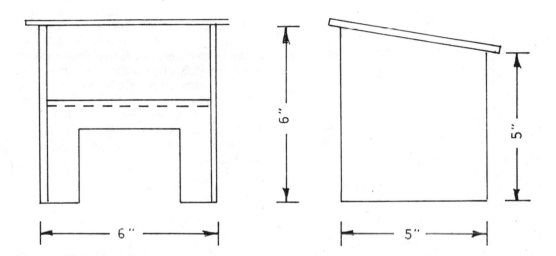

fig 1c Shed with hayloft

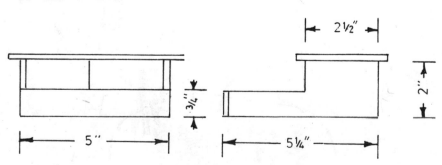

fig 1d Pig sty

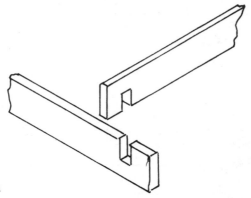

fig 2 Detail of fence join

fig 3 Pond

Farm Animals
(shown in colour on page 87)

These farm animals are intended as an alternative to shop-bought plastic ones. Cut them out of ⅜in birch ply in exactly the same manner as the Noah's Ark animals on page 54. The outlines have not been drawn in proportion to each other; you will want to decide for yourself what relative sizes to make them. The fox has been included because he roams in the surrounding fields and the children play games keeping the fox away from the chickens.

fig 4a Farm animals

fig 4b Farm animals

fig 4c Farm animals

116

GARDEN GAMES

(shown in colour on page 70)

My children found these toys great fun to play with in the summer, so much so that I made a miniature set for them to play with indoors. For this reason I have left the size variable so you can choose how large you want the finished toy to be. The drawings are given in the form of a grid and the scale can be adjusted as necessary.

Toytown Croquet Set
I am not very artistic so I used compasses to draw almost all of the figures. This will make it easier for you to copy. Use any thickness of timber, even hardboard is adequate. I used ⅛in ply for the miniature set and ¼in for the full size one. Make sure the holes are the right size for the balls you are using.

fig 1a Toytown croquet hoops

fig 1b Toytown croquet hoops

1 It is most important to get the size of the hole constant, so first of all choose what size of ball you are going to use. A tennis ball size for the full size set and a 1½in ball for a miniature set are good examples. Make the holes large enough for the ball to go through easily. Once the measurements have been decided, draw all figures to the same scale.

2 Cut out each figure with the fretsaw (jigsaw), following the outlines in fig 1.

3 Make a notch at the bottom of each figure to accommodate the bracing piece which is merely a short strip of ⅛in or ¼in ply that slots in the notch on the bottom.

4 Paint the figure on both sides, or even just on one side. I only painted the front and no one objected.

5 Make a mallet by taking a section of large dowelling, drilling a hole in the side and glueing in the handle which is made out of another section of dowelling. If there is a problem obtaining dowelling large enough for the mallet head, cut a piece of square wood to the required length and cut off the corners to make it octagonal.

Hoop-la

This traditional game can be played either on the ground or, if a hook is added, hung on a wall or door (fig 2).

1 Cut out the hoops first, making them any size you wish, and then make a board to the same scale.

2 Drill holes for the dowels in the board. Either leave them to be simply pegged in, which is convenient for dismantling and storing the set, or glue them in permanently.

3 Paint the hoops using a different colour for each set. This helps enormously with the scoring. Use dry transfers for the numbers on the board.

118

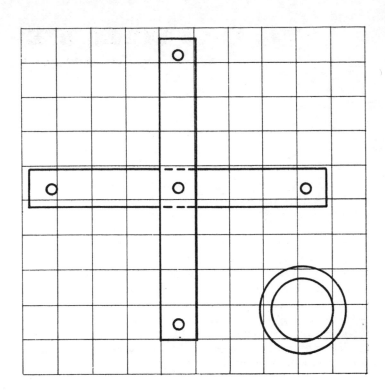

fig 2 Hoop-la (right)

fig 3 Horseshoes (below)

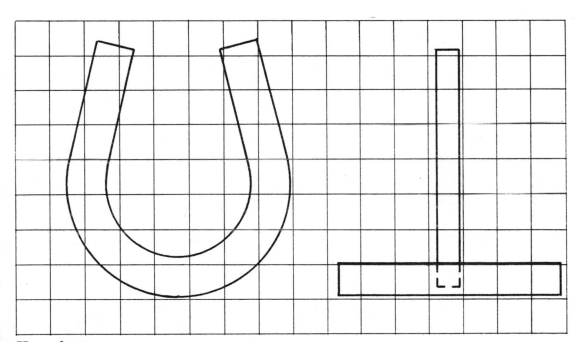

Horseshoes

This game was very popular when I first produced it. Simply cut out a pair of horseshoes (fig 3) for each child, choosing a convenient size to work with. Paint each pair a different colour. The peg can be either knocked straight into the ground, or fitted into a block of wood so that it is free standing. Score 4 points for the nearest horseshoe to the peg, 3 points for the next nearest and so on.

119

DOLL'S BED

(shown in colour on page 88)

This bed is intended for a 12in to 14in doll. If a different size doll is to occupy it, reduce or enlarge the bed as required.

1 Mark and cut out the two ends and the bed itself from ½in birch ply.

2 Cut out 4 pieces of ply 1in wide and glue and nail them on to the bed legs. This makes the legs 1in square and gives additional support to the bed — in case your children stand on it, as mine do.

3 Glue and nail the ends to the bed, and sand the whole thing for painting.

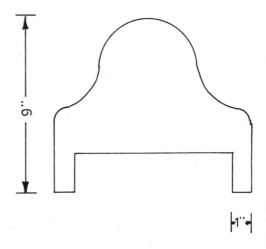

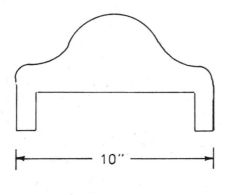

fig 1a and b Bed ends

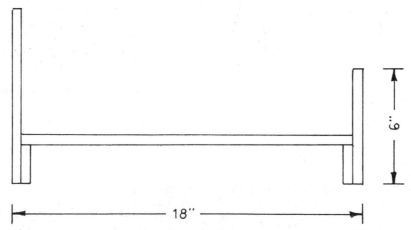

fig 1c Side view of the bed

4 The crown, heart and initials are cut from ⅛in birch ply and glued onto the bed. The small quantity of ⅛in ply required is probably best bought from a model shop.

5 The final step is to paint the bed. For the main colour I used white vinyl silk paint.

fig 1d Decorative shapes on bed ends

ROCKING CRADLE

(shown in colour on page 88)

This Rocking Cradle is made to the same scale as the Doll's Bed. I have again used ½in ply with strength in mind.

1 Cut out the two ends, following the patterns illustrated, ensuring that the rockers are exactly aligned.
2 Cut out the two side sections and the bottom, chamfering the edges of the bottom for a neat finish.
3 Finally sand down, undercoat and paint the cradle. I used white vinyl silk and a coffee colour for the shaded areas. Stick on pictures of hearts and flowers, and leave the children to make their own bedding.

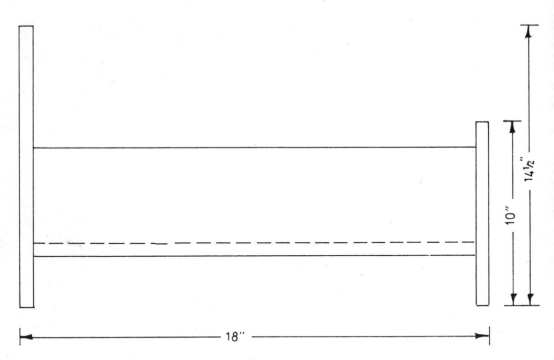

fig 1a Side view and dimensions of the cradle

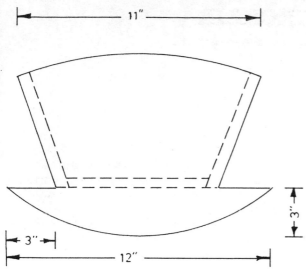

fig 1b End view of cradle showing curved rockers

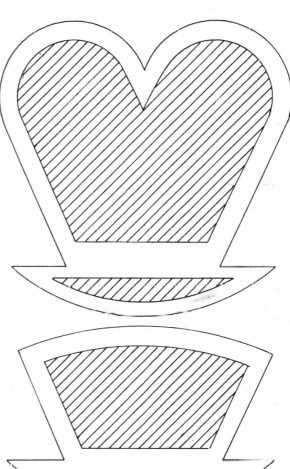

fig 1c Head board with arched areas representing decorative panels

fig 1d Decorative foot of bed

DECKCHAIR

(shown in colour on page 70)

Dolls have traditionally slept with children, joined in their games, had tea parties. As can be seen in the photograph, they also like to sunbathe, so why not allow this important member of the family a little comfort and make this simple deckchair?

There are only three sections to a deckchair but, as anyone who has tried to put one up for the first time or watched others trying to will realise, these three pieces are quite sufficient for things to go wrong. So to avoid any confusion, the first step is to identify each section:

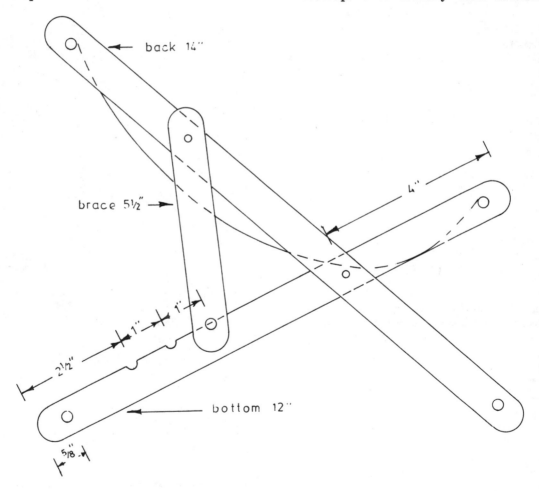

fig 1 Dimensions of deckchair: note positioning of canvas

bottom, back and brace. These three pieces fit inside each other when the deckchair is folded up. They therefore need to be different widths, the bottom being the narrowest at 5¾in, then the back at 6¼in and the brace the largest at 6¾in.

1 Cut two of each of these pieces from ¼in × ¾in strips of wood, rounding the ends with sandpaper.

2 From ¼in dowelling cut two 5¾in lengths for the bottom, two 6¼in lengths for the back, and one 6¾in length for the brace.

3 Drill ¼in holes for the dowelling ⅝in from both ends of the 4 bottom and back pieces and one end of the 2 braces.

4 In addition, drill the semicircular notches in the bottom rails. These notches can prove difficult without the aid of a drill stand. An alternative method is to cut V-shaped notches and round them out, using either a small round file or fine sandpaper wrapped around a piece of dowelling.

5 Drill pilot holes for the screws.

6 Glue the dowels in place. Then, using round-headed screws, fix the back to the bottom and the brace to the back, but not too tightly.

7 All that remains now is to fit the deckchair canvas. Glue or sew a piece of cloth 5¾in wide and 14in long around the dowelling.

My daughter's doll apparently has fair skin and requires a lot of suntan oil. If the doll you are making the deckchair for has a similarly sensitive skin, I would recommend using a plastic-type material which will be easier to wipe clean than canvas.

PICNIC TABLE

(shown in colour on page 70)

Most people enjoy the opportunity to have a barbecue or go off on a picnic, children in particular. On these occasions, however, it is imperative that their dolls join in the fun and games — and the food- so with these days in mind, I set out to make a simple picnic table.

Apart from allowing time for the glue to set and the wood stain to dry, this table may be made in less than an hour.

1 Cut thirteen strips of ¼ × ½ × 9½in wood to make the table top and the seats; two strips of ½ × ⅝ × 5in long strips for the table top supports and two strips of

½ × ½ × 9in strips for the seat supports.
2 Assemble the table top and the seats by fixing the strips of wood on the supports allowing ¼in spaces between each strip.
3 Cut out the four legs. Each one is ½ × ½ × 5½in. Glue and nail the legs in place.
4 Cut two braces, ½ × ½ × 4¼in and glue and nail them in position.
5 Place the table on a level surface and mark around the bottom of each leg with a pencil laid flat on its side to give the correct angle for the base of the leg.
6 The table may be either stained or varnished.

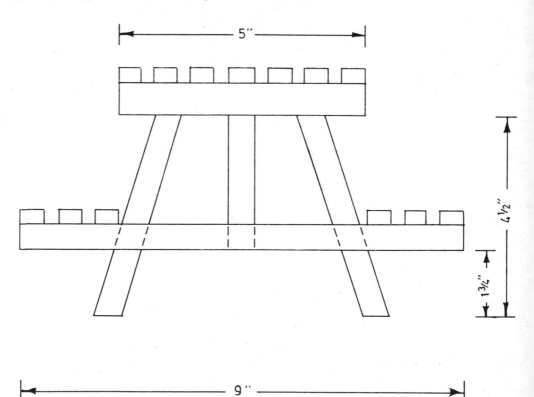

fig 1a End view of picnic table

126

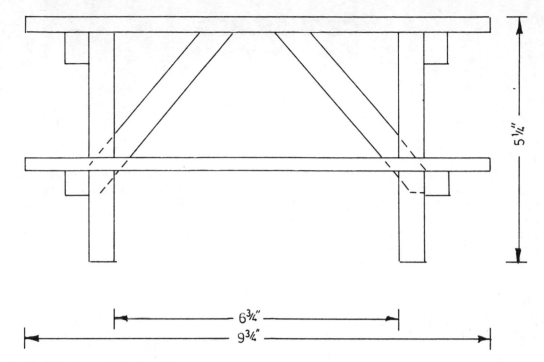

fig 1b Side view of picnic table

CRIB MOBILE

(shown in colour on page 88)

When Mum is busy knitting baby bootees and jackets and Grandmother is making cuddly dolls by the truckload, there is no reason for Dad to be left out. How about making one of these Crib Mobiles? The two shapes I have chosen are a dove and a stork. You can easily mix n' match them. I chose to use a 10in diameter brass ring to hang them from, but there is nothing wrong with cutting the ring out of the wood; shapes can still be cut from the internal waste.

fig 1a Dove shape

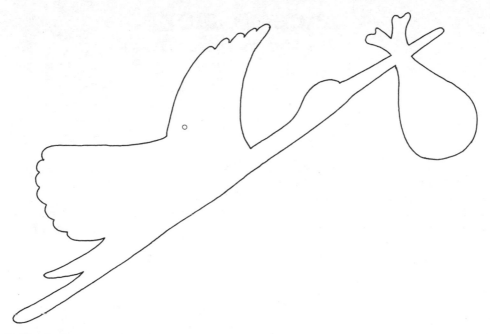

fig 1b Stork shape

1 Cut out as many shapes as you require (this depends on the size of the ring you are using) from ⅛in ply.
2 Drill a very small hole for the thread, and sand the shapes. It is important to position the hole accurately.
3 Use invisible nylon thread, which is very strong, to hang the shapes from the ring. Varying the length of the thread to make the birds 'fly' higher or lower creates a more attractive appearance.
4 Use three or four lengths of thread to hang the ring from the ceiling. Make sure that the mobile is secure, as the baby won't be very pleased if it's woken by a flock of doves dive-bombing the crib.

LACE-UP SHOE

(shown in colour on page 70)

This type of toy helps children develop their co-ordination between hand and eye. It also teaches them to do up their shoe-laces; after my daughter mastered it there was never a pair of shoes in the house with the correct laces. Making the shoe could hardly be easier, and it can be any size you like.

1 Draw the outline shape on to a piece of ¼in ply and cut it out.
2 Drill ¼in holes for the laces.
3 Paint on an undercoat and then draw on the design. This design is copied from my daughter's training shoes.
4 Paint the shoe.
5 Hide your own shoes.

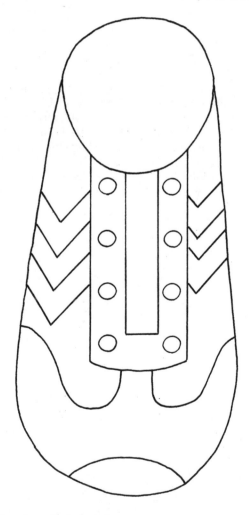

fig 1 Design on shoe taken from training shoes

SCRAP WOOD

(shown in colour on page 88)

If you have made any of the toys in this book you are more than likely to have some scrap wood left over. Rather than throw it away, why not make some small toys out of it, either for your own children or for friends.

Some of the ideas for using up waste, already found in the book, include making soldiers and wooden animals. They may be made out of any thickness of wood and to any scale. Wooden letters are also an excellent way of using up waste, as you can see from the wooden letters on the jacket. Either use the outlines provided or trace around the letters of the alphabet, using an ABC book as a guide, and cut the letters out. Children can learn to match the letters up to those in the book, they will become familiar with different styles of letters and they gain confidence from drawing around the wooden blocks and learning to put words together. Numbers may be used in the same way. Use a child's counting book for the original patterns and gradually introduce different shapes and sizes until the child is familiar with any number, however it is written.

Any of these ideas — animals, soldiers, alphabet letters or numbers — can be dipped in water paint and used to create patterns, hopefully on paper!

a b c d e
f g h i j k
l m n o p
q r s t u v
w x y z

ABC
DEFG
HIJKL
MNO
PQR

S T U V
W X Y
Z 1 2 3
4 5 6 7
8 9 0

INDEX

Page numbers in italics indicate colour plates